LIFE THROUGH THE LENS OF A DOCTOR-BIRDER

ALSO BY JOHN FITCHEN

Birding Portland and Multnomah County

LIFE THROUGH THE LENS OF A

DOCTOR
BIRDER

A MEMOIR

JOHN H. FITCHEN, MD

INKWATER
PRESS

PORTLAND • OREGON
INKWATERPRESS.COM

To my sons, Matthew and Marty
Great guys, fully fledged

TABLE OF CONTENTS

PREFACE

I noticed it first at parties: people I hadn't seen for years (or ever) would come up to me and say something like, "Hey, John—I saw this little brown bird in my backyard the other day. It was very active—coming to the feeder for a second or two, then disappearing into the shrubs. What do you think it was?"

It mattered not whether I could identify this nondescript bird; what mattered was that people presumed that I could. Birding, it seemed, had become part of my persona. It reminded me of interactions early in my medical career, when it was presumed that because I was an MD, I knew all there was to know about medicine.

Gradually I realized that birding and medicine have much in common: both are part of nature; both are extraordinarily complex; both grow and change; both are exciting and fulfilling; both are competitive; both reward study, observation, curiosity, and persistence; and both have much to do with people.

In fact, this book is largely about people. People I've

encountered in seventy-three years on planet Earth. Exceptional people, ordinary people, leaders, followers, friends (many), enemies (a few)—but human beings all. In the writings that follow, I will share with you stories of those who have touched my life, and how I've viewed these people and experiences from the perspective of a doctor and a birder.

The critical role of people makes sense for the doctor part—you can't do medicine without other people: patients, families, colleagues, nurses, staffers, students. Part of the joy of academic medicine (the career path I would follow) is teaching eager young minds to appreciate the beauty of the human machinery, to marvel at its magical interactions, its exquisite self-regulation, its ability to recover from insults internal and external, its stunning capacity for adaptation. Medicine is all about people.

But what does birding have to do with people? A lot. Seeing and identifying a new species, a "lifer," is fundamentally exciting—but it is even more so if shared with other people. Birders love nature. We are attuned to the extraordinary diversity of avifauna. We are excited by the subtleties of morphology, behavior, and habitat; the fact that birds brighten our lives with song and color; the joy of an unequivocal sighting after an arduous trek; the realization that chance favors the prepared mind; the shared experiences etched in memory because a certain special bird recalls the moment—the time and the place and the people. That shared excitement is what connects us—what drives birders to go where we go and do what we do.

I am, indeed, a doctor and a birder, but my life has been more than medicine and birds. It has been interspersed with some rousing adventures, and always there has been the comfort of family and home.

The chapters in this book are arranged chronologically, beginning when I was a young boy in Hamilton, New York, through college, medical school, training, and careers in academic medicine and biotechnology. The birding seed was planted by my father when I was a child, fertilized by a bit of competition with my older brother, and blossomed when I had more time to devote to it.

Along the way, in all the various venues, both avian and medical, I have had the good fortune to meet and work with brilliant and inspiring people—people of innovation and curiosity, of rigor, integrity, and determination—people and experiences that have shaped my life.

It is my hope that readers will come away from *Doctor-Birder* inspired to embrace their own sense of wonder and to view life through a lens that is uniquely theirs.

John H. Fitchen, MD
Portland, Oregon
January 2019

AUTHOR'S NOTE

To give you a taste of the passion of birding—what it's like to be closing in on a special life total—I've included at the end of each chapter my personal field notes, unembellished, on the most recent birds sighted in my quest to reach 300 species in my home county, a number never before recorded. And of course, the higher the goal, the more difficult the sightings.

These notes include some birder lingo that is worth explaining up front. My home county is Multnomah, Oregon—"Mult" for short. Note that of the twenty-one new birds on my county life list that I've "ticked" (seen and checked off) since November 2010, seven are first-ever records for Mult, ten are Code-5 (five or fewer sightings *ever* for the county), and four are Code-4 (found only occasionally and not expected to be encountered every year). I have presented each description with the species name "clipped" to the bottom so that if you like you can cover the name and try to identify the bird from the description alone. Following the standards set forth by the International Ornithologists' Union, specific bird names are always capitalized, whereas generic names are not (e.g., "Wood Duck" is capitalized but "duck" is not).

Two overarching observations: since I've seen all the easy birds, finding new ones depends on 1) spending a lot of time in the field, and 2) getting tips from other birders.

You can observe a lot by watching.
– *Yogi Berra*

CHAPTER 1
DAD: BUTTERFLIES, CATERPILLARS, AND CATHEDRALS

I was eight years old and my heart was pounding. Behind our house and across the creek, a spectacular butterfly had just landed in a meadow of low grass and milkweed. I gripped my net with white knuckles and contemplated my next move. Even at my tender age, I knew right away this was not the common great spangled fritillary, but a close relative, Atlantis fritillary, coveted in upstate New York. The names always seemed reversed: shouldn't the rarer and splashier butterfly get the "great spangled" billing? Though outwardly similar, the smaller size, more intense coloration, and diagnostic black margins on the outer edge of the wings confirmed that this was an Atlantis.

The year was 1953. Back then, the rules of the game were to preserve and mount specimens to display in

Left: **Great spangled fritillary** *(Speyeria cybele)* **(photo by Jim P. Brock);** *Right:* **Atlantis fritillary** *(Speyeria atlantis)* **(photo by James Dunford)**

some prominent place as a testament to one's prowess as an accomplished naturalist. But that meant you had to catch them first. A simple round net with a two- to three-foot-long handle was used for this purpose. Two basic techniques were employed: a straight downward thrust or a lateral sweep. As a child, I took to the simpler downward thrust, but of late my father had been encouraging me to learn the sweep. I knew he would be hugely pleased and excited with my catch, especially if I could accomplish it with the sweep. Given the perch of the Atlantis in the low grass, this was of course all wrong—low-perching butterflies should be captured with the downward thrust, and high-perching butterflies should be caught with the sweep. But alas, I didn't yet understand the niceties and figured the grown-up technique was the better choice.

Disaster! The rim of the net got caught in the thick grass, and the butterfly flew calmly away, out of reach, and then out of sight. Why didn't Dad tell me when to use the sweep! I burst into tears, sobbing as I ran home, where he was mowing the back yard. I threw myself into his arms, beating my head into his chest, unable at first to speak between sobs. Finally I was able to blurt out, "Atlantis!" I was furious—with my dad, with myself, with the world.

Over time, I came to appreciate Dad's deep respect for and understanding of the natural world. He was a rigorous naturalist, and he wanted to pass that rigor along to me. I remember our times looking for butterflies with great fondness. Nearly fifty years later, a few days before he died, I wrote him a poem recalling those times together.

> I wrapped my whole hand around a single finger
> Of the tall man who walked beside me.
> He helped me find cocoons (redbark was best).
> We put them in jars on the sunporch to hatch.
>
> He taught me that fritillaries favor milkweed
> And painted ladies like to stop on thistles.
> We walked the dirt roads together, wordless but at one,
> And in "Quiet Corner" listened to the silence.
>
> Now the single finger's mine and the hand my son's.
> In easy step we walk the paths that show us Nature's ways.
> I see again through boyish eyes the simple and the
> wondrous,
> And pass to mine what came from you and ever is
> among us.

In his professional life my father was a professor of fine arts and a scholar of Gothic architecture. On the side, he was also a very clever fellow. In the mid-1960s while I was off at college, he dreamed up a plan to eradicate the eastern tent caterpillar (*Malacosoma americanum*) from a sizeable chunk of the Chenango River Valley of central New York. In its worst outbursts, this scourge could completely defoliate tens of thousands of acres of forestland.

For years in the countryside around my hometown of Hamilton, New York, the Boy Scouts had undertaken an annual project intended to slow the spread of this noisome insect. Their methodology involved burning the "tents"— either *in situ* (at branching points in the affected trees), or after infested limbs were cut from trees and consolidated for burning at a safe distance. Though well-intentioned, their effort was largely ineffectual and caused damage to the very trees they were meant to save.

Enter John F. Fitchen, III. Before choosing a strategy, he did some research. He learned that tent caterpillars lay their eggs in late summer as a cylindrical nodule wrapped around small twigs, each "cluster" containing 150 to 350 eggs. The eggs are laid near the tip of the twig so that when they hatch in early spring, the tender, succulent leaf buds will be close at hand.

Armed with this critical knowledge, Dad set about attacking the tent caterpillar population in and around Hamilton—no fireworks, no sawing off of limbs, just a simple rotation of the wrist to snap off twigs and drop them to the ground away from the budding leaves, out of reach of hungry hatchlings. He estimated that over the course of five or six years of winter weekends, he destroyed over a million eggs. If that seems unlikely, do the math: 5 years, 10 outings per year, 100 egg clusters per day, 250 eggs per cluster or 5 x 10 x 100 x 250 = 1,250,000 total. In a similar time span, the Scouts might burn a couple hundred tents, damaging the trees in the process.

Not wanting to sully the good name of the Scouts, Dad was quiet about his results, telling only family and close friends—and, off the record, the Boy Scout authorities, hoping they would adopt his approach. Alas, little egg balls don't have nearly the thrill of burning tents and I fear his advice went unheeded. However, by the time he had finished his work, there were very few caterpillars left to be found and destroyed.

Dad eradicating tent caterpillars 250 at a time

When I learned about Dad's feat of eradicating the caterpillars, I was struck by his economical approach to a seemingly complicated problem. How do you wipe out more than a million tent caterpillars without harming the trees they occupy? It turned out, once you knew the secret, it was a fairly simple task. Research, contemplation, and persistence yield results.

I took note.

In 1953 and again in 1959, Dad took a sabbatical from

Colgate University to study the Gothic cathedrals of Europe, especially those in France. On the first of these trips, he brought the whole family—Mother, eldest son Allen ("Skip," sixteen), middle son Leigh (fourteen), and me (seven). We purchased a VW Bug convertible, every square inch of which was precisely occupied by us and our luggage. Being the youngest and the smallest, I was inevitably relegated to the middle back seat—what my boys would call the "bitch seat." Though seemingly disadvantageous to me, this family dynamic worked in my favor—Skip and Leigh had little interest in cathedrals, especially when the alternative was checking out *les jeune filles* who congregated in the cafes lining the central square. Mother orchestrated their comings and goings, leaving me with Dad to explore the impressive buildings that were the focus of the towns and cities we visited.

The purpose of the four-month excursion was to assess, firsthand, the manner in which these extraordinary twelfth- to sixteenth-century buildings had been erected. Unlike the scholars who had written extensively about the esthetics of cathedrals, Dad wanted to determine how they were actually constructed, how stones were placed upon stones, how vaults and buttresses absorbed and redirected the weight of the heavy lead roofs.

He came armed with an array of assets to apply to the task—though he spoke little conversational French, he could read medieval French and was a trained architect and tenured professor of fine arts. We would track down the building supervisor and explain, largely by way of sketches Dad drew on the spot, what we wanted to see. This meant that I got to clamber around the inner features of the building, up and down spiral staircases, on top of the vaults, under the lead roof, among the arches and buttresses, literally touching the elements that made it all stand up. Some of these on-site sketches were subsequently transformed into the formal illustrations that appeared in his book *The Construction of Gothic Cathedrals* (Oxford University Press, 1961). The drawings I liked the best had ropes. These simple elements provided a sense of scale, action, and a work in progress.

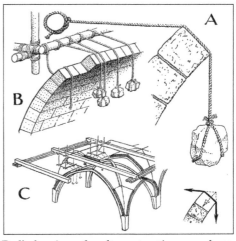

Dad's drawings of vault construction procedures, from *The Construction of Gothic Cathedrals* **(Oxford University Press, 1961)**

Impressed by the quality and detail of the sketches, the superintendent would take us wherever we wanted to go. Through the magic of Dad's drawings, we became privy to the interstices of the greatest cathedrals of France—Chartres, Reims, Amiens, Beauvais, Rouen, and Notre Dame, to name a few. My favorite was Vézelay, a Romanesque/Gothic cathedral constructed mostly in the twelfth century. It was made of local limestone. Lit by the plain-glass windows at the east end of the building, the white limestone produced a dramatic glow in the apse behind the altar.

Having seen the spectacular stained-glass windows of Chartres, where one is uplifted by the glory of luminous color, I was amazed that an equally compelling effect

The nave at Vézelay Cathedral looking east to the apse (iStock.com/RomanBabakin)

could be produced by the plain windows of Vézelay.

Later in the trip we travelled to England to visit relatives, and took a side trip to check out Salisbury Cathedral. In keeping with the style of British cathedrals, the dominant feature of this one was a very tall spire at the crossing, dwarfing the rather modest vaults rising above the nave. While others were drawn to the massive tower, I walked in, looked up, and declared to my family, "What a short church!"

The indelible images of 1953 were reinforced six years later when we returned to France, this time as a threesome (my brothers were in college) to refine observations and fill any gaps. Though I would have preferred to mingle furtively with the girls in the cafes, I was drawn nonetheless to the magnificence of the cathedrals. Some five years after that, as a freshman at Amherst College, I took the fine arts survey course, the mid-year segment of which featured extensive coverage of Gothic architecture. To help us prepare for the test on this topic, our professor hung pictures of a series of cathedrals on a wall of the art building. While others struggled to memorize the images, looking for irrelevant clues (is the chandelier on the left or the right? are there twenty or thirty rows of seats in the nave?), I walked along the hall ticking off the cathedrals with ease, pointing out the diagnostic features that differentiated one from the next. I aced the test.

FIELD NOTES

A diving duck discovered on 1/2/11 by Dave Irons off Broughton Beach during the Christmas Bird Count. The bird was accompanied by Surf Scoters and scaup. Dark overall, but not jet-black—thus, most likely a young bird. Thin, upwardly concave bill with beginnings of yellow at base of bill. Light face, dark cap.

Postscript: This first-ever sighting in the county had a material effect on the Count—it came to a screeching halt while everyone raced to Broughton Beach, hoping to tick the bird on their county life list.

Bird #280. **Black Scoter**

[Mult First Record; Code-5]

CHAPTER 2
HAMILTON

Maine? *Augusta*. Nevada? *Carson City*. Kansas and New Mexico? *Topeka* and *Santa Fe* (Atchison, Topeka, and the Santa Fe railroad—a convenient mnemonic from a childhood song for remembering the state capitals of Kansas and New Mexico). Typical chitchat at the Fitchen dinner table when I was growing up in the 1950s and '60s. We tried to stump each other with toughies like North Dakota (Bismarck), Iowa (Des Moines), Washington (Olympia) and—ha, ha, so easy it was hard—Oklahoma (Oklahoma City), the only state where the name of the state is recapitulated in the name of the capital.

When we grew tired of geography, we would switch to, say, US Presidents (the toughest being the run of Millard Fillmore, Franklin Pierce, and James Buchanan, sandwiched between Zachary Taylor and Abraham Lincoln; and Benjamin Harrison, squeezed between Grover

Cleveland and Grover Cleveland). The idea was for the boys—Skip, Leigh, and me—to trip up our parents, but with a medieval scholar and a high school English teacher to contend with, we had little chance. And woe betide the kid who fumbled his grammar or syntax. Mother would simply not abide it.

My mother, Elizabeth Nelson Fitchen, was almost universally known as "Betty." The exception was my dad, who called her, for reasons lost in the fading glimmer of time, "Jochick." She was a classy woman—bright, well-educated, worldly, engaged, and accomplished. She was petite, standing barely five feet tall when stretched to her maximum height. She *always* wore high heels, smoked Phillip Morris cigarettes (three per day, with a stylish holder—like her favorite president, FDR), and drank gin martinis. She had an exceptional ability to keep dinner on hold—hot but not over-cooked—during cocktail hour, while she and Dad had a "splash" (another full drink) before repairing to the dining room.

She had a busy, productive life. While raising three boys, she established and developed the town's first nursery school in conjunction with St. Thomas' Episcopal Church and served on the Beautification Committee that redesigned and enhanced the village green and the Broad Street storefronts. She was particularly active in the New York State League of Women Voters, so it came as no surprise to us when her name was put forth as a candidate for the position of president of the board of directors of the New York State chapter. She told us this was unimaginable and far beyond her capabilities, and besides, no woman from upstate had ever held this post. But I saw a twinkle in her eye when she reflected on it, an excitement in her voice when she spoke of it. As a fourteen-year-old sophomore in high school I could tell she would go for it.

"Okay, Mom," I told her, "I'll bet you $1,000 that before you die you will take the position of president of the New York LWV board of directors." We wrote it up and everything—signed, sealed, and delivered. Of course I didn't have that kind of money, but clever fellow that I was, I constructed the bet in a no-lose fashion—if she took the job, I got the $1,000; if she didn't, I didn't have to pay until she died, at which time I would inherit the money anyway. As it turned out, she took the job, performed admirably during her tenure from 1961 to 1963, and happily paid off the bet.

My best friend in high school was Eric Dahn (pronounced "Dan"). We sat in class together, did homework together, went on camping trips together, worked at the golf course together, and, most especially, played sports together. We were essentially the same size, a fact that had consequences: it meant that we were always paired up in one-on-one drills. Take, for example, a football tackling drill. One of us would be designated the tackler, the other the ball carrier. We would lie head-to-head on our backs, jump to our feet at the coach's whistle, march two steps away, pirouette 180 degrees, plunge toward each other at full speed, and collide with maximum force. The last man standing won the drill. I always got the worst of it, because he was, well, *tougher*—a force, an uncompromising competitor.

To wit, at the beginning of the season we were all

With Eric (*right*) when the standard was "leave the campsite better," before "no-trace camping"

issued a mouth guard to protect our teeth. Eric, whose jaw ground with non-stop intensity and unrelenting determination, went through a mouth guard at least once a week, while mine lasted the whole season. Or take wrestling. He was a master of a hold called, aptly, the crucifix. In this maneuver, he would wrap his body around mine in such a way that he was scrunched up and I was stretched out. He would then gradually lengthen his body, painfully applying pressure to my fully extended neck and legs. Unwilling to give in to my best friend, I would spend entire practices stretched in the crucifix with tears streaming down my cheeks. When we had meets with other schools, he would compete at the 145-pound weight class (our natural weight), and according to the rules of the sport I would have to move either up a class (to 152, where I'd face bigger, stronger opponents), or down a class (to 138, which I would do by restricting fluids, and then wrestling weak and dehydrated).

Or consider President Kennedy's fitness program, which included, among other exercises, squat-thrusts, designed primarily to strengthen the quadriceps. In this drill, you drop to your hands, keeping your feet under your body, thrust your legs out behind you, pull your legs back under you, and stand back up. I went first and collapsed after 85 squat-thrusts. Eric came next, blew by 85, passed 100 with no sweat, and finally stopped at 120 because he was bored. The next day I had to walk up the stairs backwards with my knees locked so as to avoid stressing my quads and collapsing. Ah, the joy of high school sports.

Eric and I worked during the summers on the grounds crew of the Colgate University Seven Oaks Golf Club. His dad ("Dahnie") was the greenskeeper at the club. A key part of his job was to get feedback from the membership on potential revisions of the course, ostensibly to improve the quality of play. This meant hanging around with members at the pro shop and occasionally having a drink with them at the bar. They would gather around and lobby for changes to the golf course, often adamantly, and usually seeking adjustments that would favor their individual style of play. The problem was that there were as many changes requested as there were styles of play, no way for Dahnie to make everyone happy.

We grounds-crew grunts were oblivious to these high-level matters. But we knew there was trouble whenever we heard the ill-fitting bed of Dahnie's ancient pickup truck blamming across the rickety little bridge that spanned Payne's Creek near the equipment shed. The banging was audible all over the course, and was always followed, from whatever quarter, by the high-pitched lament of Bernie (one of the grounds crew old-timers). "Jeeeeezzusss Chroisst, this sounds bad!" he would shout. Once across the bridge, at a vantage point from which he could see most of the course, Dahnie would leap from his truck, flailing his arms, pointing every which way, screaming at the top of his lungs. All of us on the crew could see his mouth moving, but from two or more fairways away couldn't hear a thing he was saying. We knew he was signaling, but knew not where he wanted us to go or what he wanted us to do to respond to the patrons' latest demands.

The first summer I reported for work on the grounds crew, I was instructed by the regulars that I should "twitch" the sixth fairway first thing. They told me that twitching involved the use of long bamboo sticks which were swept back and forth to break up the dewdrops that had condensed on the grass overnight. As a result, the balls of early-morning golfers would roll straighter and longer. When they thought I was out of earshot, the old-timers (Bernie, Fergus, and "Swamp Rat") cracked up in gales of thigh-slapping laughter. "Uh, I think I've been had," I whispered. Turns out that twitching is a time-honored practice used to prepare *greens* for mowing with special close-cut machinery. A green could be twitched in ten minutes; twitching an entire fairway would take days.

We worked from seven in the morning to four in the afternoon, Monday through Friday—and sometimes, during dry spells, we worked at night as well, watering the parched fairways and greens. Nowadays, watering is highly automated, but in the early 1960s much of it was manual, and involved turning sprinkler heads on and off with coordinated timing and patterns that avoided a drop in village water pressure. This meant driving the tractor from sprinkler to sprinkler, winding slowly through the course. And all of us knew that to get the tractor out of the shed, you needed to know where the keys were hidden from the public—a piece of information that would prove crucial in a subsequent adventure.

The summer after I graduated from high school, I got a job at the Morgan Horse Farm, owned and operated by the American Management Association (AMA). The farm was located at AMA's 140-acre White Eagle Banquet and Conference Center on Lake Moraine, three miles north of Hamilton. I didn't ride the horses—I fed, watered, and cleaned up after them. Part of their diet, especially through the winter, was hay grown on the farm. Accordingly, I got to participate in the annual ritual of "haying"—collecting the food that would sustain the horses through the cold months ahead.

One day later that summer, the decision came down to harvest the hay. It would be cut and raked into rows on one day and baled and collected on the next. Nervous about forecasts of thunderstorms, the manager impressed upon us the urgency of the timing. He had waited and waited, maybe too long—we had to go now! The hay had been cut and there was no turning back. Haying is a tricky call, he explained, a dance between ripening and rain. You have to wait long enough to let it mature—but the longer you wait, the more likely it is that the hay will get wet. And if the hay gets wet, you run the risk of it rotting, and even spontaneous combustion.

The forecast for the day of baling and collecting was thunderstorms "late." So starting at six in the morning, six of us set forth to get the hay baled, collected, and secured in the barn. We were arrayed across the field, with Murray, the supervisor, driving the baler. He was followed by a dump truck with a crew of five—the driver, three bale hurlers (left, right, and rear), and one receiver (me) up in the bed of the truck. From first light until after dark, with thunderheads looming in the southern sky, we moved purposely up and down the field. I was barraged with unwieldy bales, incoming from left, right, and behind. My job was to "catch" the bales and stack them as neatly as possible in the bed of the truck so it would carry the maximum load. When the truck was full, we drove quickly to the barn (hoping not to lose any bales on the way), dumped the bales in the center aisle—no time to unload by hand, no time for a stylish wagon, no time to stack bales—and zipped back to the field to renew the cycle. Finally, ushered in by a clap of thunder, the rain roared in at 9:30 p.m., but the hay was safe. Exhausted, drenched in sweat, we sat atop the huge pile of bales in the barn. Stacking could wait until tomorrow. Then, magically, Murray appeared with a case of cold beer. Never has a cold beer tasted so good.

Later that summer, after barhopping the taverns of downtown Hamilton, I suggested to Eric that we check out "the dam." He said he was bushed and needed to get to bed. I decided to check it out anyway.

Situated at the south end of Lake Moraine (AMA was at the north end), the dam that formed the reservoir was a storied place frequented by teens looking for some late-night action. I drove the three miles up East Lake Road, hooked a left at Spillway Road, and soon arrived at the narrow parking area at the base of the dam. No cars—a bad sign. No action. As I tried to turn around on the narrow roadway, I—uh-oh—backed up a little too far. My VW Bug slid down into the muddy ditch at the side of the road. I was stuck and alone. There were no homes nearby—and even if there had been, I wasn't about to go knocking on doors at two in the morning. Then I had an idea: if I could get the tractor from the golf course, I could use it to pull out the car.

As I ran the three miles back to the golf course, it dawned on me that I didn't know where the key to the new shed was hidden. The previous year they had built a new shed in a new location and I no longer knew where the key was sequestered. But I had an ace in the hole: it so happened that Eric lived on East Lake Road, just across from the golf course. He would know where to find the new key.

The problem was how to wake Eric without waking his parents. Dahnie was a sound sleeper and therefore not a factor. But Eric's mother, Lib, slept lightly and kept a five-battery flashlight on her bedside table—not so much to provide light as to provide a weapon should she encounter an intruder. Moreover, their bedroom was directly over the garage. They didn't bother to lock the garage door, because there was no way a would-be interloper could open it without waking Lib and facing the five-battery flashlight. She was a lovely lady, a real sweetheart, but not one to be messed with by invaders of her turf. To know the fierce side of Lib Dahn was to understand her son on the football field and the wrestling mat.

In an effort to avoid an encounter with Lib's flashlight, I decided to go to the back of the hillside house and throw pebbles at Eric's window. But like his dad, Eric was a sound sleeper, and the pebbles didn't wake him, especially after an evening of doing Hamilton's bars. Fearing that I would rouse Lib if I persisted with the window, I decided to try the equally perilous garage route. I returned to the driveway and ever so gently inched the garage door up about a foot. I then lay on my back, wriggled headfirst under the door into the garage, crept up the basement stairs past Lib's open door (!), and on up another flight of stairs to Eric's room. I plopped solidly on the side of his bed, gave him a blast of beer breath, then held a finger to my lips. Coming out of deep sleep, he tried to absorb what was going on.

"Don't wake up," I whispered, "just tell me where the key to the new shed is."

"Eye level, back side, second pine to the right as you face the door," he mumbled.

Before he could comprehend what was happening, or offer help, or (god forbid) turn on a light and wake up the household, I was gone—down the stairs, past Lib's open door, through the garage, under the door, and on to the golf course and the shed. I found the key right away, on the second tree to the right, and tooled up East Lake Road on the tractor. In no time, I chained the car to the tractor's trailer bar and pulled the car out of the ditch. I was feeling pretty smug having completed my task without incident.

Then I realized I had two vehicles and one driver. I was getting tired, so I decided I'd try and tow the car to the shed and avoid the three-mile trek back to pick it up. I shortened the chain in hopes of keeping a "tight leash" on the VW. But even so, there was enough play that whenever the road sloped downward, which it often did, the car's front bumper would slam up against the back of the tractor. As I calmed down and slowed down and learned how to keep the bumper up against the trailer bar, the banging subsided. And before I knew it, I arrived at the shed, parked the tractor, and returned the key to its hiding place.

I thank the universe that the county sheriff or a state trooper didn't happen by during my tractor-pull adventure down East Lake Road. Even more remarkable, I'm amazed that I managed to slide by Lib Dahn without getting a five-battery flashlight wrapped around my skull. To this day, the Dahn family refuses to believe this tale. No way could I have made it through the garage without waking Lib, they say. I'm here to tell you I did.

FIELD NOTES

A smallish woodpecker seen at SE 16th and Linn on 2/21/11. I saw the bird three times in Garthwick on the other side of the county line. A molting juvenile with bold facial pattern and two light bars through the otherwise brown face. No red on top or back of head. Extensive white barring on back, giving the bird an overall light appearance. Bold white wing patches. The key sighting for Mult was brief but satisfactory for a location determination. As I approached, it flew from a maple on the Clackamas County side to a fir on the Multnomah County side. I saw clearly the undulating flight pattern and the sudden dive and landing. It was woodpecker-shaped and a bit smaller than a robin.

Bird #281.
Yellow-Bellied Sapsucker

[Mult First Record; Code-5]

CHAPTER 3

LANAKILA

Growing up on the East Coast, I spent my summers from ages nine to fourteen (1955 to 1959) at a boys' camp: Camp Lanakila, on Lake Morey—near Fairlee, Vermont. I've since learned that the typical camp experience on the West Coast lasts only a week or two, but at Lanakila you stayed for the whole summer. One of the camp's features was the so-called Viking Awards. Patterned roughly after the Boy Scouts of America's Eagle Scout program, Viking Awards featured four levels of achievement (*Loki, Tyr, Thor,* and *Odin*) in categories like swimming, boating, camp crafts, nature, hiking, sailing, riflery, and tennis. Completing the curriculum in each of these levels would lead eventually to the awarding of a Viking Honor. At the higher levels, and especially at the Odin level, the hurdles became very difficult.

There was, for example, the "deep-water shakeout."

The requirement was to paddle a canoe into water deep enough to be over your head, capsize the canoe, let it fill with water, empty the canoe, and paddle it back to the dock. Sounded simple enough until you pondered how to remove the water from the canoe when you were in water over your head. It was accomplished by going to the back of the water-filled canoe (while keeping track of your paddle), kicking like crazy to get it moving forward as fast as possible, lunging up over the stern and pushing down with all your might. This would force the bow up, spilling water over the gunwales as it rose. This maneuver might have to be repeated several times, but eventually enough freeboard was created that you could move to the side of the vessel and slosh water, with a rhythmic motion, up through the gunwales and into the lake. Finally, you scrambled up over the side and paddled (if you still had a paddle) back to shore. Over the years I had tried and failed many times to pass this arduous challenge.

In another particularly daunting requirement, you were given an axe, a log of firewood (soaked for two hours in water), and a single stick match. No paper, no twigs, no Boy Scout juice (lighter fluid). Thus armed, you had to make a pot of water boil over. The proper procedure was to split the log into smaller and smaller pieces, thereby exposing the dry inner layers of the log. You would select the driest piece, split it down to pieces small enough to light with a single match (or so you hoped, because if you miscalculated you were dead). When I felt ready to tackle this challenge, I produced some nice splinters and some dry kindling-sized pieces, and decided to risk the match. I got the splinters and kindling started before I realized I needed more than a flame: I needed a full-fledged fire capable of making a pot of water boil over. So I shifted into high gear: splitting up the remaining dry wood, adding it to the fire, and blowing on the glowing embers until the pot boiled over.

Getting a Lanakila Odin, at least for a thirteen- to fourteen-year-old, is a big deal. When I started at Lanakila, the honor had been bestowed on only seven boys since the camp's founding in 1922. I became the eighth, making an overall frequency of one every four to five years. As of 2017, ninety-five years since the camp's founding, sixteen campers have received the award. I'm proud to be one of them.

At Lanakila's ninetieth-anniversary gathering with my Viking shield; the emblems on the back of the dragon represent Loki, Tyr, Thor, and Odin

A fun part of Viking Awards was following everyone's progress over the summer. On the porch outside the dining hall there was a big wall filled with the names of all 127 campers and the steps they had completed toward their Loki, Tyr, Thor, or Odin status. This information was periodically updated by filling in little boxes on the massive chart with a magic marker. In the summer of 1959, when I was closing in on meeting the requirements for Odin, my fellow campers would stop by the chart to check out my progress. It was going to be close. With only two weeks to go, a six-day canoe trip through the Rangeley Lakes in western Maine, and a project on the Nature Trail to complete, I had little time to attempt, yet again, the deep-water shakeout. I contemplated skipping the Rangeley trip, which wasn't a Viking requirement, but it was supposed to be fantastic and I figured I could manage. I finished the Nature Trail project before we left for the Rangeleys and practiced the shakeout while we were there.

Upon returning, I headed directly to the boathouse and selected a canoe. Campers at the adjacent swimming docks climbed out of the water and watched as I paddled out into a deep part of the bay. Sailboaters luffed their sails. Counselors, including two in a nearby evaluation/ rescue boat, stared intensely as I moved through the steps. Capsize—no problem; go to the stern—no problem; make headway—no problem; mount the stern—no problem; shake out the remaining water—no problem; clamor into the canoe—no problem; keep track of your paddle— damn! Where is it? Oh, shit—this is my last chance! Miraculously the paddle appeared on the other side of the canoe, close in, easily reached.

Kids on the swimming docks cheered, counselors clapped, campers at the tennis courts up the hill shaded their eyes to try and figure out what all the commotion was about. The counselors in the rescue boat told me that had I not secured the paddle I would not have passed, but that I had recovered nicely and all was well. They gave me a slip with a checkmark by "Deep-Water Shakeout" and the words "Lanakila's Latest Odin" penciled in at the bottom. Slip in hand, I was wafted by fellow campers up to the dining hall, to the wall, to the woman with the magic marker, to the final box on the progress chart. I'd made it with three days to spare.

Part of the ritual of becoming an Odin is to spend a night in the woods on the eve of receiving the award. It isn't exactly a requirement—it's an expectation, a vote of confidence from the entire camp that as an Odin-to-be you are competent and capable of handling yourself in the woods, alone and in the dark. So the evening before the award-conferring council fire, I hiked the mile up to "The Cabin," a broken-down structure with a caved-in roof, started a fire in the clearing (with a single match), warmed some soup for dinner, laid out my poncho and sleeping bag on a cozy bed of pine boughs, stoked the fire one last time, and went to sleep.

I learned later that Mrs. Carol, the camp director, walked up to the cabin soon after dark. She found me asleep, breathing deeply, in rhythm with the crickets and the whip-poor-wills. She had intended to talk to me about the gravitas of getting my Odin, the meaning of this milestone in the context of Lanakila and of the life that lay before me. But she said I seemed so clearly at peace, so in tune with nature, doing what an Odin was meant to do on a night alone in the woods, that she decided not to disturb my sleep.

Of course, she couldn't have known that "being in tune with nature"—to the point of spending a couple of grueling weeks at the edge of the North American continent in order to look for rare birds, which was what I would do decades later—was precisely the life that lay before me.

Later, at the darkest hour of the night, when light and heat had left the fire, I was brought suddenly to full alert by a spine-tingling cacophony of grunting, snorting, panting, and braying—some horrific beast was close at hand. My just-turned-fourteen-year-old body shook with fear, but I managed to do two things: silently unzip my sleeping bag (so I could get out quickly if I had to) and open my trusty Swiss Army jackknife (to create at least the illusion that I could defend myself against whatever fire-breathing monster was coming my way). I thought about making a dash back to the camp, but that was unacceptable—everyone was counting on me, everyone was with me. I must not let them down.

As the terrifying noise continued, I clutched my knife as tightly as I could and wondered what I might be up against. Maybe it was just counselors trying to test my mettle. But no—even Lanakila counselors couldn't make sounds like this: primal, visceral, grotesque, driven by the brainstem. Finally, after what seemed like hours of staring into the murky darkness, I drifted into an uneasy sleep.

When I awakened in the morning, I found the knife still clutched tightly in my hand and had to peel my fingers off the handle to let it go. Through the rest of the day, my right hand was useless, locked in the shape of a claw.

With help from Mrs. Carol and some long-term counselors, I subsequently pieced together what had happened. This was 1959 and thousands of trees still cluttered the forest floor in the aftermath of hurricanes Carol and Edna, which had hit the area back in August and September of 1954. What I had been frightened by was a large buck making its way down to the stream below the cabin, struggling to negotiate a pathway over, under, and around the downed trees, and crashing and snorting its way through the fallen trunks as it fought to reach the water.

As a young teenager, I was transfixed by this experience in the woods, riveted by the frightening sounds of the night, proud to have survived with nothing worse than a claw for a hand. I doubt I could do any better today. Hell, I flat-out couldn't do it today. And from that night alone in the woods, I learned a life lesson. Scary things are going to happen in your life. Keep your head. Hope for the best, prepare for the worst, and keep your cool.

Later in life, as an executive in a publicly traded biotech start-up, I was often confronted with swirling rumors that would cause our stock to plunge or soar. I learned that the most important thing was to stay calm: most of the rumors were unfounded. And the few that were actual problems could often be resolved with modest adjustments.

In other words, it turned out that Bigfoot wasn't stalking me in the woods—but even if he had been, it didn't matter.

FIELD NOTES

A striking sparrow-sized bird found by Andy Frank and Tait Anderson at Vanport wetlands on 4/26/11. A young bird with stunning orange-red belly, throat, and head. Dark-gray back, tail, and nape. Black line from nape to eye, narrow dark lores. Short, thin, all-black bill. Flycatching behavior.

Bird #282.
Vermilion Flycatcher

[Mult First Record; Code-5]

CHAPTER 4
AMHERST

With tears welling up, I watched the green Oldsmobile 88 drive slowly around the quad and exit onto Route 9. I stood in front of James Hall—where, with help from my parents, I had unloaded my worldly possessions into a second-floor corner dorm room. My roommate, Bruce Grean (later known as "Goody"), was nowhere to be found, but there was evidence that he had arrived—a wooden "GET BENT" sign hung on the wall, and Stan Getz was making music on his RCA record player.

Not knowing what to do, I wandered aimlessly across the quad to the War Memorial that overlooked the playing fields at the bottom of the hill. I would report to these fields with the rest of the freshman football team the next morning. A fellow freshman stood nearby, taking in the vista that stretched to the Holyoke Range in the distance. He looked a lot more confident than I felt.

"Hello, I'm Tom Weiskel from Newton High School," he said. "Who are you?"

"I'm John Fitchen, from Hamilton High School in upstate New York," I replied.

"How many students in your senior class?"

"Forty-nine."

"And what was your rank?"

"Two." I paused. "How many in your class?"

"Eight hundred."

"And what was your rank?"

He didn't say a thing—just slowly raised a single finger. *Oh god*, I thought. *I'm in way over my head.*

I returned to James Hall, where this time I *did* find my roommate—a tall, lanky, friendly looking lad groovin' to the music. He said he was from Erie, Pennsylvania. We didn't exchange class ranks. We decided to walk down the hall and meet our neighbors. The name tags on the door of the second room on the left read "Jonathan Lehrman" and "Richard LeFrak." The door was open, so we walked in and introduced ourselves.

"Nice to meet you, I'm Jon Lehrman," said the one nearer the door. I turned to the other one and said, "Then you must be Rich."

"Rich?" he replied. "The richest." (In fact, his family ran the LeFrak Organization, Inc., one of the largest real estate firms in New York.)

LeFrak turned to Jon. "Hey Si"—apparently "Si" was Jon's nickname—"this guy looks a lot like the Gootch, don't you think?" LeFrak was gesturing at me but apparently referring to a high school buddy in the Five Towns area of Long Island.

"He does—the similarity is striking," replied Si. They

turned to me and chimed, "We hereby pronounce you 'the Gootch' from this day forward." It's a name that has stuck, and that I will doubtless take to my grave.

At ten the next morning I reported to the playing field as instructed. Having been the quarterback and captain of my high school football team, I was excited and hopeful that I might have a chance to do well in this aspect of college life. This wishful thinking was quickly dashed when Coach Wilson told us to circle up for a pre-practice team meeting. He told us that ninety of us had signed up for freshman football, and that seventy of us were captain, quarterback, or both on our high school teams. I was quickly relegated to fourth- or fifth-string running back, and at the end of the season (during which I actually scored a fifty-yard touchdown—amazing), I decided not to go out for the varsity team in the fall, although I later joined the team as a junior and senior.

A week after my humiliating introduction to freshman football, classes began. The marquee course—part of the mandatory core curriculum and a rite of passage for incoming freshmen—was English Composition 1. Everyone called it just "English 1." The course was all about writing—or rather, *thinking* and writing. We were asked to write three two-page papers a week. The assignments were rather obtuse—one three-week segment was devoted to "exploring the difference between correct and 'correct'" in a variety of situations. Confused? So were we.

Part of what made the agony special was that it was

shared by the entire class—every single freshman. We would collectively wrack our brains trying to think of something, *anything*, cogent to write. We would pace the halls, often through the night, and finally settle in at our Smith-Corona typewriters with little time to spare and, despite all the pacing, nothing much to say.

The class after our first assignment was due, Professor Townsend strode into the room carrying a stack of papers and set it down on the desk at the front of the room.

"I want to commend you," he said, tapping his finger on the stack. "There are twenty-five students in this class and I received twenty-five perfect themes." We all breathed a sigh of relief—and then, with little ceremony, he picked up the stack of papers and dumped it in the wastebasket by the desk. "Let's see if you can do better next time. Class dismissed."

The criticism that rained on us over the course of the semester was unrelenting and unmerciful, with marginal comments like "Huh?" or "No," or, worst of all, "Mayonnaise." Like soldiers in boot camp, it seemed we needed to be broken before we could be fixed. But after some threshold, some accumulated dose of mayonnaise, after enough wallowing in the goo, we began to understand the importance of clarity, of getting it straight in the brain and transporting that essence to the printed page. I passed English 1 and, well into English 2, I began to get comments like "OK," "Not bad," and ultimately, miraculously, "I see" and even "Interesting." And in the end, of all the courses I took in college and medical school, all the preparation for a career in academic medicine, none was more important than English 1 and 2; these courses helped me to write and speak with clarity, and that was central to all that would follow.

First semester sophomore year I had to select a major. I had no clear idea what I wanted, but I knew I liked people and biology, and reasoned that these two areas of interest intersected in medicine. The rules stated that as a pre-med you had to declare a major tied to a specific department (usually in the sciences), and take additional courses outside your major to fulfill admission criteria of the leading US medical schools. So I majored in biology and took other necessary science courses, especially in chemistry—as well as fun elective stuff like French Lyric Poetry, Modern European Art, Shakespeare, Readings in the Humanities, Beethoven, and Michelangelo.

One of the required courses was Organic Chemistry, reputedly a sieve that filtered out weaker pre-med students. I found the material to be challenging and difficult to comprehend, but rewarding on those rare occasions when a light bulb turned on. The tests were extraordinarily difficult. I remember one midterm in which I got a 13 (out of 100) and the best kid in the class (a pure chemistry major) got a 63. I don't know how, but some guys got grades that were below zero (!). Still, thanks to the curve, I managed to get a C. The night before the final exam, I was ridiculed by my fellow pre-meds for being stuck on page eight of the 1,500-page textbook.

"I'm trying to understand the difference between S_N1 and S_N2 reactions," I told them. "It's pretty cool."

"But Gootch," they said, "the test is in the morning, less than ten hours away—and you're only on page eight."

When it came, the final exam was a classic. It consisted of seven questions of which we were to answer five, each counting 20 points. I read the first question. I had no idea. But that's okay, I thought, I only have to answer five. I read the next question—no idea. Question number three—no idea, but that's okay, I can still get an 80. When I finished reading all seven questions (none of which had to do with the difference between S_N1 and S_N2 reactions), I still had no idea, so I read them all again—nothing, no light bulb, not even a glimmer. And time was running out.

In desperation, I barfed onto the page anything I could think of, no matter how tangential, and handed it in with a silent prayer.

Two days later I was contacted by the chemistry department secretary to set up an appointment with Professor Kropf, the director of the Organic Chemistry course. "Oh shit," I thought. "I must have failed. Why else would he be wasting his time with me?" I asked the secretary what it was about, but she was evasive. I would have to wait until the appointed hour to learn my fate.

The next morning, facing Mr. Kropf in his modest office, I realized once again how impressive he was. He just plain looked smart—because, well, he just plain *was* smart.

"What happened on the final?" he asked. "You were doing so nicely, one of the better pre-meds, and then you completely collapsed on the final. What went wrong?"

I mumbled something about an unorthodox approach to studying for the test, and slouched down in the chair.

"Well, given your crash on the final, I'm afraid the

best I can do is give you an 82 for the course," he said, shaking his head.

Did I hear that right? An 82? It was all I could do to contain my joy and relief. Straightening in the chair, I managed to exhale. "Sorry to disappoint you. I enjoyed the course. I learned a lot from the final." I practically ran back to the fraternity house to tell my pre-med buddies the incredible news, and to gloat over my 82. We tipped back a few that night.

I went out for varsity football junior year but, not having participated as a sophomore, I failed to move up much in the depth chart. Basically, I was the best of the scrubs and accordingly played the role of the number one running back for each week's upcoming opponent. The final week of the season was special—the critical game was a show-down with our archrival, Williams College.

Head Coach James "Smokey Jim" Ostendarp called us together at the beginning of the week and told us in his thick Baltimore accent, "Awright now, this week we play Williams College, the most important game of the year. It is a rivalry that dates back to 1884, known as the 'Biggest Little Game in America.' Now, Williams College has a fine running back named Eddie Wing, the key to their offense, their leading scorer. So we've put a bright yellow jersey on Fitchen boy here and he's gonna be Eddie Wing. Now I want you to focus on one thing and one thing only: we're gonna *get* Eddie Wing. We're gonna hit him high, we're gonna hit him low, we're gonna get ... Eddie ... Wing!"

By the end of the week I was battered and bruised, but the strategy worked—we won the game 42 to 8 (in Williamstown) and Eddie Wing gained only 61 yards (compared to his season average of 154) and didn't score a single point. Not bad. They also serve who only ride the bench.

There is a remarkable footnote to this story. Fast forward fifty years and I get an email from a former post-doctoral fellow of mine, Mike Riscoe, now an internationally recognized malaria researcher, who had read an editorial on toxoplasmosis in *Clinical Infectious Diseases* by Edward Wing, MD. Mike wondered if this could be the same Eddie Wing I had referred to in the story I had told at some lab party many years ago. I said I didn't know but thought it plausible and would check it out. There was an email address for Dr. Wing with the editorial, so I gave it a try. I explained who I was and, if he was the right Eddie Wing, how I had spent a week pretending to be him in the fall of 1965.

I heard back almost immediately. "Thanks a lot for reminding me of our defeat and the score of my final football game. All I remember is cold and mud and not getting any traction. The good part of that weekend was my future wife, Rena Rimsky, now Rena Wing, was my date."

I replied, "Tell Rena that all great women go to Amherst–Williams games, so I'm not surprised you met there." We exchanged brief bios that indicated we had both had careers in academic medicine—he at the University of Pittsburgh and Brown, and I at UCLA and Oregon Health & Science University. Small world.

Spring semester of senior year I had a dream schedule: T-2 and Th-2; that is, Tuesday and Thursday, both at two in the afternoon. Both were seminar courses with no papers, no tests, and no final—the grade was determined by class participation. Each course was taught by a distinguished professor. The first was Senior Honors in Biology with Richard T. Yost, Jr. (who later would become President of the American Association of University Professors). Professor Yost was wildly popular with students, admired for his broad interests and adored for his common touch, doling out one-liners like "never pipette with your middle finger, you never know where it may have been." The second was American Intellectual History with Henry Steele Commager, the celebrated American historian who rallied support for Adlai Stevenson in 1952 and 1956, and John Fitzgerald Kennedy in 1960.

The day of the week that these courses were held proved to be important. Professor Commager's course was held on Thursday, the day after what we called "Wednesday Night in the Voom Room." This ritual at the Beta Theta Pi fraternity house was a well-oiled tradition meant to foster serious discussion—well, it was *meant* to be serious, but more likely was an activity we hoped would score points with our dates. From the tap in the basement, we would bring up "drawers" of beer (wooden desk drawers full of paper cups full of beer) to Room 6 on the second floor—the Voom Room. To participate in this co-ed gathering, you had to abide by one simple rule— LBDNT, or "look but do not touch." As the evening wore on, this rule was followed (more or less—mostly less), and the intellectual quality of the discourse also dropped a notch or two. We talked and laughed and sang into the wee hours, with little thought of what the morning (and afternoon) would bring.

I managed to arise in time for the first meeting of Professor Commager's seminar but had not found the time to study the assigned reading. Though diminutive in stature, the professor was imposing—regal, almost. He was also quite presbyopic, and sported a pair of pince-nez to see things near at hand. He carried a clutch of 3x5 cards containing our names. He would pose a question, shuffle through the cards, select one at random, bring it in close to his glasses, and call out a name.

I sat in fear, trying to be invisible. But sure enough, my name came up on the second question, something like "What do you make of the influence of Adlai Stevenson on American geopolitical thought, Mr.—uh—Fitchen?" He squinted over the top of his pince-nez.

"I'm sorry sir, I received the assignment late and haven't had time to do it justice," I managed to croak out. "I'll try to do better next time."

He peered down the table. "Mr. Fitchen, are you chewing gum in my classroom?"

"Yes, sir—sorry sir, I'll take care of it right away," I replied. I pretended to swallow the offending nugget, but actually just stashed it inside my cheek, reasoning that I wouldn't be so unlucky as to be called on twice. Sure enough, three questions later, my card came up again and I had no answer. But that was nothing compared to the opprobrium visited upon me by the professor.

"Mr. Fitchen, are you *still* chewing gum in my classroom?" he spewed, like fire from a dragon. "How dare you! Take care of this now!"

I did. But in the aftermath of Wednesday night's

activities in the Voom Room, I managed to drag myself to class only once over the remainder of the semester, and was never called on again (at least as far as I know).

At the end of the semester I received my grades, and there it was: History—Incomplete. I was not quite sure what that meant, but sensed that it was not good. I had just been accepted to the University of Rochester School of Medicine "pending graduation from Amherst College." With a growing sense of panic, I tracked down my buddies to get their advice. The universal wisdom was "Talk to the Ghurst"—"the Ghurst" being Alan Havighurst, a classmate and fraternity comrade. He was the third of three brothers to go to Amherst and had an uncle who taught history at the school. The Ghurst was reputed to know everything there was to know about Amherst College.

He listened closely to my tale of woe, thought for a minute or two, and then gave me his advice. "Okay, Gootch, here's what you should know and a strategy that just might work. Professor Commager is an avid sports fan—especially rugby. Go meet with him. Tell him you're the captain of the rugby team (which you are) and that you were preoccupied by activities related to that position, including getting to practice early, conflicting with class time, that you broke your collarbone in the Wesleyan game (which you did), and that the pain was aggravated by prolonged sitting (which it was, at least for a few days). And didn't you have to wear a harness and a sling for a week or two? Dig those out of the back of your closet and put 'em back on for the meeting."

I reported to Professor Commager's office the following day fully harnessed and slung, and set forth my

About to get clobbered in a rugby match with Wesleyan (*left*); because of a broken collarbone and Professor Commager, I got a free ambulance ride (*right*) and graduated from Amherst (photos by Jim Gerhardt, Amherst College Archives & Special Collections)

case, following the script provided by the Ghurst and adding the conditional acceptance to med school. I told him how much I had enjoyed his class when I could be there, and how I wished that could have been more often.

"I'm sorry, Mr. Fitchen," he said. "This is all well and good, but I simply have no recollection of you ever being in my class."

In desperation, with nothing to lose, I played my last card. "Don't you remember, sir—I was the one chewing gum in your classroom," I said.

"Oh, that was *you*. Yes I do remember. I'll take this under advisement. Check with the Registrar's Office tomorrow. This meeting is over."

Tomorrow finally came. I trudged to the Registrar's Office and, barely able to breathe, asked for a copy of my transcript. Bingo! There it was—a 70 in History. A passing grade with room to spare. I would graduate. I would go to med school. The future looked bright. All was well.

To this day I am grateful to Henry Steele Commager—grateful for his willingness to see the big picture, grateful for his humanity, and grateful that he cut a break for a desperate senior.

FIELD NOTES

Found by Jay withgott and reported to me by Andy Frank and Shawneen Finnegan on 10/6/11. A small all-white egret less than half the size of the associated Great Egrets and a little more than half their length. Much "busier" in its foraging routine than the Greats. Dark, slender bill with yellow lores. wings all white, including wing tips. Slender long neck when extended. Legs lighter than bill; feet not visualized. No obvious plumes, so probably a juvenile bird.

Seen again today, October 7, from about fifty yards—compared to about half to three quarters of a mile yesterday. key findings on closer study are as follows: bright-yellow feet, legs yellow in the back, dark green in the front. Bill gray and black with obvious yellow lores. Also confirmed the absence of plumes, indicating that the bird is, indeed, a juvenile.

Bird #283. **Snowy Egret**

[code-5]

CHAPTER 5
SNOW SCULPTURES AND VIRGINITY

During my freshman year at Amherst, my parents were headed to Europe for a month, and had let me know that I was welcome to use the house while they were abroad. They encouraged me to visit so I could check that all was well, and they were excited for me to see the fancy white-pile carpet they had installed in the living room just before their departure. I asked if they would hide a key so I could get in, but they said it wasn't necessary because, they reminded me, they never locked their doors—or at least they never locked the back door, even when they were out of the country. Such was their trust in the citizens of Hamilton. What a place, what a time.

As it happened, Amherst winter break fell in the midst of their time away. I called Eric Dahn (my best friend from high school, then a freshman at Trinity College in Hartford, CT) and gathered up roommate Goody Grean, and we headed for Hamilton. Eric had checked ahead and discovered that Colgate University Winterfest was to be held that weekend. All three of us were eighteen (the legal drinking age in New York at the time), so we would have no trouble gaining access to the parties on fraternity row. Part of the Winterfest event was a snow sculpture contest. As we bounced from party to party, we walked by some impressive works in snow and ice, but none so striking as the offering of Phi Gamma Delta, a massive rendering of Cerberus, the three-headed dog that guards the gates of hell.

As the beer-drenched weekend began to unfold, we invited some Colgate guys to stop by the house for an impromptu party to sample my parents' liquor cabinet. The sole requirement for entry was that one of us "knew" you—a stipulation that soon became more of a loose guideline than a rule. Among the drop-bys were three young women from Cazenovia Junior College, and we soon found ourselves ensconced with them in the master bedroom.

Just as things were warming up, there was a tentative knock at the door. Some kid I had never seen before informed me that there was a girl waiting for me at the back door. I told him I was busy, but he persisted, telling me that she said it was very important—that she must talk to me right now. I was reluctant to leave the bedroom and the steamy prospects with the girls from Caz. I could only imagine what Goody and Eric might do with the two-on-three ratio. But when the kid cupped his hands under his chest and mouthed a big WOW, curiosity and libido prevailed. I strode down the stairs, weaving through the crowd (where had all these people come from?) and headed to the back door.

And there was Candy McCoy (definitely not her real

name), a high school acquaintance noted for her stunning figure and "liberal attitudes." She looked me in the eye and breathed the words I had been waiting my whole life to hear:

"Wanna do it?"

My mind raced. Was this a trick question?

"Me?" I managed to croak. "Okay. Follow me. There's a bedroom in the basement."

I checked the contour of my wallet, fingering the circular ridge permanently embossed in the leather from years of carrying my "be prepared" condom. With fumbling hands, I unrolled it as carefully as I could ... and *then* I put it on—or so I thought. Seconds later, it came off, as did I. For all the waiting, all the wondering, all the anticipation, the reality was, well, disappointing. Wasn't it supposed to last longer? Was this the *denouement* of years of fantasy? Could I have gotten her pregnant? I had to talk to my buddies. They would know what to do—right?

I bid Candy goodbye and returned to the party on the main floor. It had progressed. There had to be at least a hundred kids chugging beer, downing shots, and smoking cigarettes. I climbed upstairs to rejoin Goody, Eric, and the girls from Caz. I wanted desperately to talk to my friends about the simultaneous high and low of losing my virginity—but not in front of the girls. We drank late into the night—I in an attempt to suppress the alarming thoughts that were running through my brain, my buddies in hopes of doing the deed with the girls. I failed, they failed, but thank god, a week later Candy got her period—a bullet dodged.

Late the next morning I eased gingerly out of bed, checked my buddies (sound asleep), and noted the absence of the Cazenovia contingent—all was quiet. I stumbled down the stairs hoping to scare up a jar of instant coffee in the kitchen. On my way, I glanced into the living room. Holy shit. The once-immaculate white carpet was plastered with cigarette burns, flicked ashes, and smoked-down butts. I thanked god the house hadn't burned to the ground, but that didn't change the catastrophic condition of the rug. I trudged back up the stairs to get reinforcements.

As Eric and Goody surveyed the damage, they just kept shaking their heads. "This is bad," they said in unison. "Very bad."

Eric, who had a knack for such things, said we needed razor blades and Formula 409. For the next six hours we worked to restore the damaged carpet. We used the blades to tease out the divots, applied 409, then worked up the pile and combed it over to obscure any residual pockmarks. There were over 200 scars (we counted them). The result wasn't perfect, but it was a huge improvement. We thought it might even go undetected, although there remained four or five pesky lesions in the sofa cushions. The cushions were apparently made of a different kind of fabric, with little or no pile. As a last resort, we simply flipped the cushions over and hoped for divine intervention.

When Mom and Dad returned from Europe, I dreaded their first call—would they have noticed the doctored wounds in the rug, the obvious burns in the cushions? When the call came, I held my breath, but there was no mention of either carpet or cushions. I suspect they knew, and that I wasn't as clever as I thought—but they said nothing.

Ten year later, when they decided to put in a new rug, I confessed. They said they hadn't noticed any of it, but there was no doubting the spots on the cushions when we flipped them over. They told me no harm done, they still loved me. I had dodged another bullet, more or less, and reaffirmed in the process what wonderfully kind and understanding parents I had.

Fast-forward to March 1967. I was now in my senior year at Amherst, a card-carrying member of the Beta Theta Pi fraternity. Seemingly out of nowhere, the college announced it would host a winter festival that would feature a snow sculpture contest. This was rather odd in light of consistently mild winters with modest snowfall in most previous years.

As luck would have it, more than a foot of snow fell on the village a week before the contest. The event was billed by *The Amherst Student* (the college newspaper) as "the first winter festival in recent years," although none of us had heard of it personally or from friends in earlier classes. It was named the "Bacchanalia"—alcohol-charged and, by today's standards, politically incorrect. But this was 1967, and the contest included a first prize of two kegs of beer. That attracted the attention of the Betas, a fun-loving band of fraternal brothers who were customarily on the margins of everything—but who were soon to be front and center in the college-wide contest.

A week in advance, in the newly fallen snow, a handful of Betas developed a theme—and, more surprisingly, a plan—to build a sculpture that would make a statement. Recalling Colgate three years earlier, Goody and I suggested that we make our own Cerberus. In addition, someone suggested there should be a boat with partying passengers and a portal spanning the River Styx. Paul "Bunnsie" Bunn, who had snow sculpture experience from high school, said we would need lumber to form the structure supporting the heads of the massive dog and hell's gate. A squad of scroungers was deployed to procure the necessary materials, and what began as the effort of a handful of shivering visionaries gained momentum as the week wore on.

Progress was slow at first, amounting to little more than the accumulation of three amorphous mounds of snow. But gradually, as the concept emerged and the image sharpened, the labor took on a new urgency. By Thursday an around-the-clock effort involving nearly every brother was in full swing. Betas showed up on the side lawn of the house, prepared for the chilblains of working barehanded in the cold. Classwork, even among the dedicated pre-meds, took a backseat. A contingent of brothers acquired lumber from whatever sources were "available." Others built wooden frames. Hitherto unknown artistic talents appeared out of nowhere as new design elements were added. As the work progressed, the origin of the artistic vision became blurred—it seemed to become a mystical work of art created by the collective wisdom of the entire brotherhood.

Endless hours of shoveling, packing, and spraying with a garden hose produced a display worthy of Fine Arts 101. Playing on the Betas' bad-boy reputation, Digby Clapp, the only classics major in the house, provided the last-minute title, the *coup de grâce*—"Facilis Descensus Averno" ("The Descent to Hell is Easy").

The sculpture was the runaway winner of the contest, and the two kegs of Russell's Package Store's finest brew.

Cerberus guarding the gates of hell

Instantly, hours of soaked shoes and frozen hands were forgotten. Beta faculty adviser (and later college president) Bill Ward, clearly relieved that Beta had actually done something worthwhile, observed that our work was simultaneously ironic, compelling, and self-deprecating. He sent the fraternity an additional keg with a note that read, "To the best and brightest on campus."

The brothers gathered on the porch roof on the south side of the house and watched the parade of admiring gawkers driving by on Route 9, many of them just missing being rear-ended. The three kegs were consumed forthwith as we basked in the glory of our prizewinning effort.

FIELD NOTES

A pair of sparrows found on 4/9/12, off Swigert way (near Troutdale Airport) by Jay Withgott. Small, with small bill and relatively long tail. Overall drab gray-brown sparrow about the same size as an accompanying Clay-colored Sparrow. Streaky crown, nape, and back, thin complete white eye-ring, clean breast and belly. Light colored legs. The birds did not vocalize.

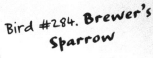

Bird #284. **Brewer's Sparrow**

[Code-4]

CHAPTER 6

MEETING ELLEN

She was walking along the far side of the room, decked out in her red-and-white striped pinafore. She didn't need the uniform to stand out—there was no doubt, she was the one: jet-black hair, great figure, drop-dead gorgeous. And she looked smart, too. She was a candy striper who volunteered at Strong Memorial Hospital, where I was about to start my second year in med school at the University of Rochester. I had seen her walk through the cafeteria periodically during my first year but had not mustered the courage to get within radar range. Now, as she disappeared out the door, I resolved to make a move next time I saw her.

I had returned a few days early, because two class-mates (Peter Martin and Jonathan "the Bear" Reynolds) were remodeling their apartment and had asked for help. They would supply the beer and beef, and the rest us would provide the labor. Envisaging a good venue for future parties, a group of us agreed to pitch in.

Peter and the Bear were well-known throughout the medical center: Peter's father owned a cattle farm and had provided his son and the Bear with a full semester's worth of beef. As a result, their intake for nearly six months had consisted exclusively of meat and beer—no fruit or vegetables or other sources of vitamins. They'd developed fissuring and dry scaling at the corners of their mouths (cheilitis), a characteristic of pre-scurvy—the first such cases in over fifty years at the medical center, and in New York State as a whole. They were being treated with limes, just like British sailors ("limeys") in days of yore. And the rumor was that their therapy was being dragged out so that all the med school community could see their lesions when everyone returned for fall semester.

Another classmate, Ira Shoulson, had also showed up to help with the remodeling. He was one of the top students in our class, but he had a reputation for fixing guys up with unattractive dates—a malediction he contests to this day. He told us that his girlfriend Audrey's roommate had returned to school early and was available that night. He wondered out loud which lucky guy would like to take her out. There was a chorus of groans and laughter.

"No way, Ira, your reputation precedes you," we chortled in unison.

"No, guys—this is different. She's foxy, a real knockout. It's different this time."

He begged us to step up to the plate. Finally, I relented and agreed to take her out, but stipulated that I wouldn't go to the trouble of bathing or changing.

"This girl's getting me as is, Ira. That's the best I can do."

When I arrived at the dorm and knocked on the door, I had a brief sense of foreboding as the door opened slowly, haltingly, and finally all the way. And there she was—my privately lusted-after candy striper. I could only imagine what was going through her mind as she checked me out—hair disheveled and full of sawdust, T-shirt pitted out, a quart bottle of Genesee Cream Ale dangling from my hand. Internally I was kicking myself. How could I have blown this so completely! After a year of wanting to meet her, I couldn't possibly have made a worse impression on the vision that stood before me. I decided to plow ahead. I think I was already in love.

"Ah—are you Ellen, Audrey's roommate?" I blurted out. "I'm John, Ira's friend. I apologize for my appearance and my, uh, fragrance. Is there some way we can start this over? If I had known it was going to be you, I would have done better."

She looked me up and down. Her frown deepened as she looked me over, but under it was a twinkle in her eyes. Maybe I had a chance—maybe there was hope.

"You talk like you know me," she said. "Have we met?"

"Not exactly," I said, "but I've been admiring you from afar at the hospital cafeteria, walking through in your candy striper outfit. Would you like to go to an apartment-christening party? It's a work in progress, but we're hoping to crack bottles of champagne over one or two of the bed frames. Oh, and two of the students have scurvy with physical findings. Is that a plus? They're considered real rarities. You don't get to see a case of scurvy every day, and I can show you two of them in the same room."

When we got to Peter and Bear's apartment, we slipped quietly in. It was so crowded we were lucky to find a spot together on the floor. For the next six hours we sat nose-to-nose, deep in conversation, singing "Mockingbird" loud and off key along with the others. I managed to catch Ira's eye and told him *sotto voce* that his reputation had taken a major turn for the better. Ellen and I talked and sang and danced till the wee hours of the morning, wanting the night to never end.

I learned that she was a senior at Rochester, Jewish, from Long Island, daughter of a physician, broadly interested—her college majors had included chemical engineering, biology, math, linguistics, and art history.

In the years to follow, this proved to be perfect preparation for running an interior design business (go figure), which she did with great success for over thirty years. Then again, it's not so surprising when you consider the capacious mind required to be a top-notch residential designer. At the peak of her career, Ellen would work simultaneously on as many as twenty projects. Each of these would include up to five rooms, and each room would contain ten or more major variables (furniture pieces, fabric selections, window treatments, floor coverings, light fixtures, kitchen appliances, bathroom fixtures, electronic devices), and each of these variables had its own variables—the style and length of the legs on a custom sofa, the size and orientation of bathroom tiles, the wattage and color of lighting, and so forth. And, of course, she presented three options to her clients, so that they could ponder the selected alternatives and make informed and guided decisions. The math is staggering: 20 projects x 5 rooms x 10 major variables x multiple additional variables—thousands of data points pinging around in her brain, all at once, intersecting and interrelating to produce the perfect solution. To this day, I marvel at her talents and abilities.

When finally it was time to part that night, I asked if she'd like to go out to dinner the next night, and she said yes.

Hooray! Bravo! Gloria in excelsis! She had said yes, she had given me her number, and we were launched. I told her she should dress up, because I would be taking her to the fanciest restaurant in town (La Bamba), and I would be wearing a coat and tie, clean hair, and extra cologne.

On that second date, we both ordered steaks and I asked the waiter to bring us a bottle of Château d'Yquem, the most expensive wine on the list—and, unbeknownst to me, an extraordinary dessert wine from the Sauterne region of Bordeaux, France. The waiter stiffened and asked if he could recommend a nice red Burgundy to go with the meat so we could save the d'Yquem for dessert. Thank god I had the sense to agree. After we ate the steaks accompanied by the almost-as-expensive Clos de Vougeot from Burgundy, the waiter had us clear our palates with bread and water—and then the show began.

It was magnificent. The Château d'Yquem was dessert unto itself, and even better when accompanied by some chocolate bonanza that La Bamba had cooked up just for us. The waiter called it "nectar of the gods." Years later when we were married and had become lovers of French wine (and could still afford it), we would laugh and cringe when recalling this story. The Great Growths of Bordeaux and Burgundy have since soared beyond our means—even though our means have increased substantially.

About a month later I brought Ellen home to Hamilton to

meet my parents. Without any fuss, Mother situated us in separate bedrooms (no big deal—we could walk). Dad and Ellen hit it off from the start. He was dumbstruck by this gorgeous young woman who was headed to Columbia University to study early Christian and Gothic art history, and she was snowed by his deep understanding of these topics. He kept disappearing to fetch another volume of Viollet-le-Duc's ten-volume *Dictionnaire Raisonné de l'Architecture Française du XIe au XVIe Siecle*, published between 1858 and 1868. She was also disappearing, gradually but steadily, behind the growing stack of books. He would open one of them and say something like, "As of course you know from volume IX of Viollet-le-Duc's *Dictionnaire*, early forms of Gothic vaulting were relatively simple, generally quadripartite."

Ellen ponders her next move at the bridge table in Hamilton

Mother's turn came after dinner, when she suggested we play a few hands of bridge.

"You know how to play, don't you, Ellen?" Mother said cheerfully.

Ellen stared at me with panic in her eyes, imploring me to say something.

"Of course she does," I said confidently. (She told me later she had never played, not even once, not a single hand.)

"Great," said Mother. "Why don't you go ahead and deal, Ellen."

She took a deep breath, picked up the deck of cards, and started dealing to her right—counterclockwise! Mother tried not to flinch, but couldn't help it as Ellen plowed ahead. Over the years we would sort it out. Dad suggested he and Ellen be partners (since neither of them much cared who won or lost), and Mom and I would be partners because we did care—probably a bit too much.

Some months later, it would be my turn to feel out of place. Ellen's parents had invited me to come down to the city so we could meet, have dinner, and go to a Broadway show. I asked Ellen what I should wear.

"Whatever you feel comfortable wearing," she said. Big mistake. I figured I'd need something warm for the drive down and something casual/dressy for dinner and the show—we were going to see Pearl Bailey in the new all-black *Hello, Dolly!* And then I had this great idea that I could cover all three venues (travel, restaurant, theater) with my slick new buffalo plaid hunting jacket. When I arrived at dinner, Ellen and her parents appeared before me, perfectly turned-out New York sophisticates. The dinner was a bit on the quiet side. Could it be because of me? I noticed that her mother kept looking furtively to her right—that's where I was sitting. Mercifully, dinner was quick, because we had to get to the show. It was great—and yep, Pearl Bailey's feet hurt, she told us as an aside right in the middle of the show.

I didn't do very well with Ellen's parents and sartorial selection, and she didn't do very well with Mother and bridge, but we were both in the game, both at first base or better, and the dynamic was evolving. We liked each other a lot.

FIELD NOTES

Two medium-sized sparrows discovered by Tait Anderson along Sundial Road on 5/10/12. The birds had bold black-and-white striping on the head and face, and an unmistakable black throat. Seen in good light at close range with scope. Alternated between feeding on apron of road, and perching on fence and rusty cattle cart. Associated with a bright male Lazuli Bunting.

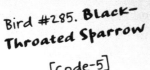

Bird #285. **Black-Throated Sparrow**

[Code-5]

CHAPTER 7
SAWADA AND SUZANNAH

During my first and second years of med school at the University of Rochester, I worked part-time in the laboratory of Dr. Louis H. Hempelmann, Chairman of the Department of Radiology at Strong Memorial Hospital. Before Dr. Hempelmann came to Rochester, he worked in the Los Alamos Laboratory in New Mexico, as part of the Manhattan Project. He was renowned for leading a seminal study of accidental radiation exposure of workers in an uncontrolled fission reaction at Los Alamos in 1946.

When he moved to Rochester, he developed and carried out a study on the long-term detrimental effects (especially thyroid cancer) of low-dose radiation therapy for thymic enlargement—a misguided practice in the first half of the twentieth century. This procedure was based on the mistaken belief that an enlarged thymus gland could lead to suffocation and sudden infant death. The thymus gland, located in the upper chest, is a specialized lymphoid organ of the immune system that is involved in early programming of T cells, which fight cancer. It is most active during neonatal and pre-adolescent periods.

The scope of the study was impressive, involving 2,657 children who had received thymic irradiation and 4,833 of their siblings who had not been irradiated. Ultimately, the study participants were followed for over fifty years—producing a total of more than 334,000 person-years of follow-up. During the study, contact was made at least six times by mail or phone. The results demonstrated that thyroid cancer incidence in the irradiated group was 18.6-fold greater than in non-irradiated siblings—a highly significant difference. This increased rate of thyroid cancer was still demonstrable fifty-seven years after exposure.

My job was to make follow-up phone calls to determine the current status of irradiated individuals and their non-irradiated siblings. Most of the time this was routine, with no new pathology to report. But once in a while, when I asked my questions about interim illness, there would be a long pause, silence, and then a quiet response: "Oh, he died three years ago of thyroid cancer." I would express my heartfelt condolences and ask if they would be willing to provide additional information for the study. They seemed somehow comforted to know that they were part of a bigger picture—that because of them and other victims, the practice of thymic radiation had been discontinued by 1960 in the US and around the world.

My time in Dr. Hempelmann's laboratory was graced by two foreign nationals—Shozo Sawada, PhD, a Japanese post-doc, and Suzannah York, a Hungarian woman (no relation to the actress) who washed the glassware. Funding was tight, so everyone performed tasks outside their standard job description. Sawada, for example, was responsible for keeping us stocked with supplies. I asked him one day for disposable pipettes and met immediate resistance. He pulled himself up to his full five-foot-four-inch height, looked me straight in the eye, and said sternly in his broken English, "John! We haven't any nickels!" It turned out that Dr. Hempelmann had just met with him to urge fiscal restraint, explaining, "Sawada, we haven't got a nickel!" Such is the beauty of idiomatic English spoken in a foreign tongue.

When I first met Sawada, I asked where he was from. He said with great pride that he was from "the most famous city in the world." Hiroshima. He told me that he lived in a suburb behind a ridge that separated it from the city center. One day when he was thirteen, he walked out of his house and looked up. A massive, churning cataclysm of light filled the sky above the city, deflected upward over the ridge. As he looked to the skies, he exclaimed, "What happened?" I told him we had something in common: he survived, and I was born on that fateful day—August 6, 1945.

Sawada was a lot of fun. He told me that golf was a prestigious and very expensive pastime in Japan (golf courses require a lot of land, a scarce commodity in that island nation), and that he would be thrilled to join a group of us on our weekly round. We rented him a modest set of clubs and a sleeve of balls and headed to the first tee. He pulled out one of the brand-new Titleists, teed it up, pulled out a five iron, addressed the ball, and took a wicked cut. Grounder to short, fifty yards, all on the ground, right down the middle. He grabbed up his bag, ran to his ball, threw down his bag, pulled out his five iron, addressed the ball, took a wicked cut, grounder to short, fifty yards, all on the ground, right down the middle. He beamed from ear to ear every time he struck the ball.

Back then, golf balls were made of a plastic core wrapped with elastic rubber bands, and covered with a tough, durable Surlyn resin coating that is hard to damage unless you're Shozo Sawada. We lost track of how many times he struck the ball, but every time he took his ferocious slash, he put another cut in its cover. By the end of nine holes (he never lost his ball and never replaced it) there was almost nothing left of the cover, and the rubber bands were spitting from the surface. One thing was certain: Sawada had a wonderful time.

Another Sawada escapade involved an excursion to the local strip joint. Like the Frestrunk Brothers (Steve Martin and Dan Aykroyd, the "wild and crazy guys" from Saturday Night Live), he wanted to see some big American girls with their big American breasts. Given Sawada's diminutive stature, when standing up at full height he measured just about perfectly to tall, well-endowed, all-American girls in six-inch heels. In this configuration, his face was level with their nipples, and bobbed up and down in sync with naked bouncing boobs. We kept tipping, he kept bobbing, and the girls were enchanted— trying, without success, to get the man to smile. But this was serious business, and he was completely engrossed. The event became known as the Bobble-Head Gala.

A particularly special time with Sawada was a spectacular dinner put on by him and his wife, Mari. They invited me, Ellen, and three of my med school classmates (the golf group) and their significant others. By this time, and especially after the golfing and strip-joint successes, Sawada had become friends with all of us. The dinner was his way of thanking us for welcoming him into our circle. But the real star of the show was Mari. She had arisen at five that morning to prepare and cook. We all showed up as instructed at five that evening, and were still going strong at eleven. Mari had not sat down the whole time. There was a steady flow of course after course of delicious food, and constantly freshened sake cups, always at the perfect warm temperature. When we arrived, Sawada had proudly displayed a huge bottle of sake—"1.7 liters," he told us. This bottle kept us well-supplied for several hours, but somewhere in the shank of the evening the supply was depleted, and a detail was dispatched to the local purveyor of wine and spirits to replenish the stock.

As the evening wore on, we eventually knew it was time to leave. To signal that awareness, we kept draining our sake cups. But as soon as we emptied them, Mari would fill them up. It took us many refills to figure out, finally, that in Japanese culture you leave your cup full to indicate that you've had enough—the exact opposite of the American custom of finishing your drink to signal it is time to go. That resolved, we had the good sense to secure a couple of cabs to take us home. We would retrieve our cars in the morning. Meanwhile, despite mass quantities of alcohol, I'm sure none of us slept better than Mari, who by my calculus had been on her feet for eighteen hours straight. (A very sad footnote: Mari died of gastric cancer a year later, soon after they had returned to Japan.)

Suzannah York, the Hungarian woman who washed the glassware, was a warm and caring human being, who, along with Sawada, brought a wonderful international flavor to the lab. She often worked later than the rest of us. In the warm months, in an effort to conserve energy, the last one to leave the lab was asked to turn off the window-mounted air conditioner. Since she was usually the last to leave, this task often fell to Suzannah. Every time she would reassure us, "I turn the air condition," and sure enough, in the morning, we would find it turned off. I can hear her say it now: earnest, responsible, and always just "turn"—not "turn off," just "turn."

Suzannah was almost always upbeat and cheerful, humming as she cleaned and sterilized the glassware. But one day she seemed down, distant, pensive. She rolled up her sleeve, touched her arm, and looked up at me with deep, searching eyes. Cautiously, gently, I asked her about the numbers tattooed on her forearm. Her response was barely audible and then she fell silent. I held her hand and waited. Haltingly, in a mere whisper, she told me her story.

In 1942, when she was a nubile sixteen-year-old, she and her parents were arrested by the Gestapo and transported to Auschwitz. When she got off the train, she and her fellow passengers were taken to a holding area, and then instructed to go through one of two gates. The men and older women (including Suzannah's parents) were herded through the gate to the left. She would never see her parents again. Today was the anniversary of that cruel separation. Her voice trailed off as she said her life had been spared by her captors—but she couldn't bear to speak of why. We hugged, and she cried. We never spoke of it again, but a bond was formed. She knew I cared. It was an honor to know her.

With Suzannah on med school graduation day

FIELD NOTES

Located at Sandy River Delta just east of the parking lot in the tall cottonwoods on 7/21/12, with Em Scattaregia and Adrian Hinkle. A male bird, it was seen mostly in shade just north of the main path. Small, plump, dark overall with deep blue undertones more pronounced distally. Short beak. Song, heard repeatedly, consisted of two or three high clear notes (*seet, seet, seet*) followed by three lower-pitched and richer notes (*sweet, sweet, sweet*).

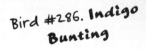

Bird #286. **Indigo Bunting**

[Code-5]

CHAPTER 8
GOLDMAN, MARROW, AND ME

The summer between my second and third years in med school (1969), I spent a two-month externship with Robert Goldman, MD, Professor of Medicine and Hematology at the University of Oregon School of Medicine (now known as the Oregon Health & Science University, or OHSU). For hour upon hour, I sat across from him at the other end of a double-headed microscope, and the "conversation" went something like this:

"John, this is a Wright-Giemsa stain of bone marrow from a patient with a rare and almost always fatal disorder called Di Guglielmo's Syndrome, or acute erythroblastic leukemia. Note the preponderance of erythroid elements, in particular immature erythroid elements. They are readily identified by their deep, rich, blue cytoplasm. Note too, the nearly complete absence of megakaryocytes and myeloid precursors, which accounts for the marked peripheral thrombocytopenia and leukopenia as well as the clinical manifestations of mucosal bleeding and systemic infection ..."

This was just a taste of my first day with Dr. Goldman, the first day of two full months at the other end of his two-headed scope. He was wonderfully calm, supportive, and non-judgmental about my meager knowledge base. He didn't speak down to me. He encouraged me to ask when I didn't know something (which was pretty much always, at least at first), and to wonder aloud how the bone marrow carried out its critical function of making blood cells—not too many, not too few, just an exquisitely balanced number. More than 200 billion red cells were churned out

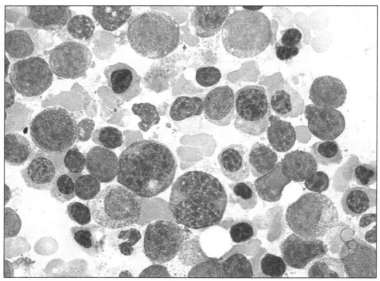

Photomicrograph of acute erythroblastic leukemia bone marrow sample (image originally published in ASH Image Bank. Peter Maslak. Acute erythroid leukemia. ASH Image Bank. 2010; Image number 4 © the American Society of Hematology)

every day—even more if called upon to increase production in response to bleeding or hypoxia.

When I looked at the erythroleukemic marrow, at the stunning colors of the cells, stalled at an early stage of differentiation, unable to produce functional red cells, I was transfixed by the captivating array of various cell types and the predominant erythroid precursors. Looking at the glorious images and the resplendent colors was like beholding the stained glass at Chartres cathedral—stained marrow/ stained glass—both with their incandescent mixtures of sapphire, cobalt, and aquamarine. And, I would later learn, it was not unlike the thrill of spotting a male Harlequin Duck in full breeding plumage. Right then and there I knew it was what I wanted to do for the rest of my professional life: to understand how bone marrow works, and doesn't work, and to teach hematology to students and house staff (medical interns and residents) and colleagues.

Not all of my time with Dr. Goldman was spent at the microscope. We saw patients in the hematology clinic, including a fourteen-year-old girl named Jeanie Perkins who had systemic lupus and was referred for evaluation of anemia. Nothing remarkable on that visit, but I would encounter her again, two years later, when she was admitted to University Hospital with a flare of her lupus.

We also made daily rounds on Dr. Goldman's hospital patients, and I got to witness his remarkable bedside manner. One Friday about halfway through the summer, we went to see a young cleric from the nearby Russian orthodox community in Aurora, Oregon. He had been admitted for diagnosis and treatment of severe macro-cytic anemia; i.e., with red blood cells that are larger than normal, but fewer in number—and much fewer in his case.

Tucked between his crisp white hospital sheets, his full beard flowing over his chest, the Russian cleric was literally as white as a sheet. We could see terror in his eyes. In an effort to assuage the man's fear, Dr. Goldman sat down on the bed, took the man's hand in his own, and, in his most soothing tone said, *"Do svidanya,"* the only words of Russian he knew. What he didn't know was that *do svidanya* means "good-bye."

The man turned even whiter, and while we all tried to reassure him, a stat page was placed for Olga in the records room—she was the only medical center employee known to be fluent in Russian. With Olga's help, we were able to communicate to him that he had a very treatable form of anemia caused by vitamin B12 deficiency asso-ciated with the thirty-day bread-and-water fast he had just completed. A faint glow of pink began to show in his cheeks.

The take-home message for me was not the faux pas with *do svidanya*, but the genuine effort on Dr. Goldman's part to find a way to provide comfort and empathy for the patients he diagnosed and treated. He tried his hardest to connect, to form a bond. Many of the patients to whom he ministered had life-threatening diseases (various forms of leukemia, lymphoma, and cancer)—scary diagnoses that engendered fear. But even up against these formidable dis-eases, he knew the power of trust and hope. His teaching to me: tell the truth, the whole truth, and tell it early on. If you don't, you will ruin the chance for trust. And find some ray of hope, some positive note to focus the effort as you move forward as a team—not some bogus miracle cure that's always around the corner, but some achievable aims like pain control, effective home support, improved strength with transfusions.

Any question I might have had about wavering from my newfound career plan was immediately answered when I returned to Rochester to begin my third year in medical school. A miraculous thing occurred—the initial six-week section in the curriculum was a focused, full-time course in hematology! From day one it was like being back in the photo-lined hallway in the fine arts building at Amherst, walking calmly, ticking off the Gothic cathedrals. Only now I was looking through microscopes and dazzling fellow students as I pointed out circulating nucleated red cells, immature white cells, megaloblastoid erythropoiesis, metastatic cancer invading the marrow—to name just a few. Needless to say, I aced the course and received gratifying feedback that reinforced my plan to become a hematologist, a goal I achieved in 1978 upon completing a fellowship in hematology at UCLA. I passed the board certification exam that same year.

The great and tragic irony of Bob Goldman's life is that he died of acute leukemia a mere eight months after he retired in March of 1994. He and his wife Irma had planned a second honeymoon in Italy in November of that year. As part of a routine change in health insurance, he had a complete blood count (CBC) performed. Part of this test involves making a stained smear of the blood to examine the morphology of the circulating blood cells.

There is an automated form of this test that is performed by a machine and produces numerical data only. Back in the summer of 1969, Dr. Goldman had stressed to me how important it was to look at the patient's smear carefully, with your own eyes—not to rely solely on the machine—in order to catch unusual cells or other useful findings that could be seen only through the microscope.

When Goldman assessed his CBC results in March of 1994, the machine reported that the white cells were completely normal. When he looked at his own blood smear, it *was* almost completely normal. Alas, the operative word here is "almost." Intermixed with the predominant normal cells were rare immature white cells—blast cells—the cells that would eventually kill him. He decided to keep this information to himself.

When he and his wife arrived in Rome, the leukemia exploded, and treatment was started with urgency. When he failed to respond, he was air-evacuated back to Portland, where treatment was continued. Despite some initial progress upon returning to Oregon, he developed leukemic meningitis (essentially leukemia of the brain) and gram-negative sepsis (overwhelming systemic infection), and died at age sixty-six on November 12, 1994—a mere two weeks after the official diagnosis of acute myelogenous leukemia (AML) was made.

He was a great man, loved and respected by the students and house staff he guided and taught. I was honored to call him my mentor. He was special—a stand-up guy, a mensch. I will remember him as an exceptional doctor, and an internist and hematologist of the first order. But above all else I will remember him as a graceful and caring human being. I miss him a lot.

FIELD NOTES

A small gull-like bird flying low over Smith Lake at the boat launch on 8/19/12. I agree with Harry Nehl's description of the gestalt—"most of the bird is behind the wings"—a reflection of the small head and long tail compared to Common Tern. Small, slim, black bill; dark at the back of the head and nape, uniform light-gray upperwings except for luminous white secondaries; all-white, forked tail. No obvious carpal bar. Overall, a small white bird.

Bird #287. **Arctic Tern**

[Code-5]

CHAPTER 9
SIGNORA IN SPILATO

The summer I spent in Oregon with Dr. Goldman (1969) was the result of an exchange program offered to students at the University of Rochester School of Medicine. We all wanted to go overseas (especially, for some reason, to Yugoslavia), but those slots always went to upperclassmen, and I had only just completed my first year. In preparation for our various assignments, a mandatory group orientation meeting was scheduled to provide us with general information and specific pointers for each of the sites.

One of the speakers at the meeting was a fourth-year exchange student from Yugoslavia. His name was Vladi. He told students headed to his homeland that all they needed, all they had to know, was an all-purpose phrase that would fit most any occasion: *Pička matarina* ("PEECH-kah mah-tah-REE-nah"). He had us say it, over and over, even if we weren't going anywhere near

Yugoslavia. Vladi just chuckled. The rest of us tucked the phrase away—for what purpose, I couldn't imagine. When we returned from our respective locations, we learned from our upperclassmen that *pička matarina* meant "fuck your mother," or words to that effect. They regaled us with tales of encounters awkward in the extreme, embarrassment beyond measure, and jaw-dropping incredulity.

A year later (1970), bride-to-be Ellen and I took a grand tour of Europe, generally travelling from city to city via Eurail Pass. One non-rail leg of the trip consisted of a ferry ride from Ancona, Italy, to Split (or, as the Italians called it, Spilato) on the coast of Yugoslavia. We arrived after dark. When we disembarked, we were surrounded by scores of sturdy women dressed all in black, shouting the word "room" in a dozen different languages. We plowed through them and headed to a nearby park, where we figured we could camp for the rest of the night.

Alas, all of the benches in the park were occupied by passed-out locals, and the ground consisted of crushed gravel—no grass, no soft places to sit or sleep. We had no Plan B, or at least none that we could afford. Then, one of the women in black appeared out of the gloom and half-heartedly called out her multilingual offering—"*camera, chambre, habitacion, zimmer,* room…" Having no alternative, we agreed on the price and shook her hand to seal the deal. It proved to be a momentous decision— our time with "Signora," as we came to call her, was the highlight of our whole trip.

We had planned to spend just one night, but our room was clean and comfortable, and "conversations" with Signora were special. We shared about twenty words in Italian, she had a smattering of English—mostly place names in the US—and we had no Croatian (well, almost no Croatian—we did have Vladi's all-purpose phrase). In what became the daily routine, Signora would rise with the sun, buy the day's food at the local outdoor market, return home to place fruits and vegetables in the kitchen sink with the cold water running over them (she had no refrigerator), brew strong coffee, then read the grounds and tell us our fortunes in measured Croatian. We didn't get much, but with enough repetition, one thing was clear: the coffee grounds revealed that we would be married within a year—a correct prediction. Another repeated theme had to do with her two sons, pictures of whom were proudly displayed on the kitchen wall. They had both been killed by the Germans in World War II. With tears in her eyes, she would speak the words over and over in Italian—*"niente Schwabo, niente Schwabo,"* or (roughly) "the Nazis are hateful, they are nothing."

During our visit we learned that Yugoslavians like to receive gifts, love to drink scotch, and always cook with garlic. I had purchased a garlic press in Paris and planned to give it to my mother, but thought it would be more impactful if I gave it to Signora, so I did. She immediately loaded it with several cloves and pushed down on the arm—nothing happened. She loaded more garlic (uh-oh), but this time pressed down with the full force of her wiry forearms. Suddenly a great gush of minced garlic exploded through the mesh. She beamed, saying, *"Strumento pratico, strumento pratico!"*

Toward the end of our stay, we asked her to show us her favorite places in Split. She arranged for a young friend with a car to transport the three of us to the aquarium and the Mestrovic Museum—she clearly was the matriarch of her block. As we moved from window to window at the aquarium, she became animated, speaking rapidly, slapping the back of one hand into the palm of the other. It finally dawned on us that she wasn't telling us *about* the fish, she was telling us how to *cook* the fish, how to prepare it, what to serve it with, when to add the garlic.

Then it was on to the museum, where we wandered among the works of Ivan Mestrovic (1883–1962), a world-renowned sculptor who was a hero in Yugoslavia. Part of his career had been spent at Syracuse University, a mere forty miles from Hamilton. I learned later that my dad had met him and was deeply impressed by the creations and the character of the artist. Signora was drawn especially to the works of the war era—soldiers and citizens with chiseled faces, muscular bodies, and defiant demeanors. She was uncharacteristically silent, moving from statue to statue with tears streaming down her cheeks. She missed her sons and wept for their absence.

Years later, on a trip to visit my brother in Chicago, Ellen and I visited Grant Park to see a Mestrovic sculpture called *The Spearman*. It precisely recalled the art we had seen in Split, and Signora's expression of fierce defiance that we saw at the museum. My guess is she would have said, "Viva Chicago. Viva America!"

The next day, our

Drawing of Ivan Mestrovic's statue *The Spearman*, Grant Park, Chicago (by Nathan Pierce)

last with this great lady, we managed to come up with a bottle of Johnnie Walker Red. Though it was only ten in the morning, word travelled up and down the street that there was a party for the beloved matriarch—*and* there was "scotty," their word for scotch. A crowd soon gathered nearby in some sort of subterranean stone anteroom, all of them talking lickety-split in Croatian, with Signora at the front with the two young Americans at her side. Toast after toast was sent our way.

"I've got to respond," I whispered to Ellen. "I've got to say something in their language."

"Don't you dare," she whispered back. "Don't you dare."

Emboldened by the scotch and figuring this would be my only chance to respond to the good wishes of the crowd, I raised my glass and said loud and clear:

"*Pička matarina!*"

The room went dead quiet. For five full seconds there wasn't a peep. Then Signora gave an almost imperceptible nod, and there was pandemonium—an explosion of cheers and laughter.

"*Pička matarina,*" they roared. "*Pička matarina!*"

And then, from Signora: "Viva America, viva New York, viva Chicago, viva Cincinnati, viva Indiana, viva scotty, *pička matarina!*"

We will never forget her.

FIELD NOTES

Discovered on 1/13/13, in a NE Portland backyard by a friendly and cooperative homeowner who welcomed birders onto her property and into her house for close-up looks at this beautiful ground-dwelling warbler. The bird displayed alert posture, prominent white eye-rings, an olive back, bold black striping on neck and flanks, white throat and belly, and a tailored head pattern with a muted orange-brown median stripe flanked by black stripes on top and back.

Postscript: The bird remained for several months. Thanks to the hospitality of the owner and the persistence of the bird, scores of birders got to tick this wonderful warbler. It is also the bird on the cover of this book.

Bird #288.
Ovenbird
[Mult First Record; Code-5]

CHAPTER 10

INTERNSHIP AND A BABY

About forty of us milled around in the dim evening light on the roof of the Multnomah County Hospital in Portland, Oregon, sipping warm beer and speculating on what the morning might bring. Freshly minted MDs, we spoke in hushed tones punctuated here and there by nervous laughter. It was June 25, 1971, and we were about to embark on a journey that would mold us into real doctors. We were about to become interns.

In 1971, the standard path after med school was to spend a year as an intern rotating through various disciplines—internal medicine, general surgery, pediatrics, ob/gyn. After this rotating internship, one chose a specialty and carried out two to five years of residency focused in that area. If med students knew upon graduation that they wanted to be internal medicine doctors, they would matriculate into a so-called "straight medicine" internship before moving on to a medical residency. That was the path I took. Nowadays, you go directly to residency after you graduate from med school. And in this time of ever-increasing specialization, many young doctors go on to a fellowship in a sub-specialty—cardiology, hematology/oncology, rheumatology, endocrinology, and so forth.

At eight the next morning, I walked onto Ward 8A, a general medicine ward at OHSU, trying to look confident. The head nurse came around the counter and greeted me. "Good morning, Dr. Fitchen. Welcome to 8A. You have two new patients—one with atypical chest pain who was admitted last night, and another with high fever and a history of lupus who is on her way from the ER. You also have two elective admissions scheduled for this afternoon. In addition, Mrs. Johnson has low potassium and needs new IV orders. Mr. Charles is scheduled for a liver biopsy at one o'clock, and Dr. Weaver would like to see you right away in the doctors' office."

Aaaarrggh! All that and a liver biopsy on my first day?

I hustled around to the doctors' office, trying to digest what the nurse had just told me. *Four new patients!* Good grief—it would take hours and hours to work them up, to review their medical records, determine current active problems, conduct a review of systems, perform thorough physical examinations, discuss each patient with Dr. Weaver (my assigned resident), agree on a plan for diagnosis and treatment, draw blood, start IVs, write the orders (for what fluid should go into the IV line), and order x-rays and other tests as indicated. *Write IV orders?* I had done that many times, but this was different. As a med student you write "orders," but they are always reviewed and countersigned by real doctors before they are carried out. This time my orders would be official—when I signed my name, the order would be an order, and the order would be carried out. *Liver biopsy?* I had seen a few, but had never done one. And this procedure had potentially life-threatening side effects, most notably laceration of the liver, serious internal bleeding, emergency surgical intervention—even death. Oh, dear.

Kathy Weaver, MD, senior resident, was a force, a high-impact doctor, stunning in the breadth and depth of her knowledge. Though diminutive in stature, she had a presence that was compelling. She was a woman of few words, but when she spoke, people listened. I found her right away in the doctors' office and introduced myself. She sized me up, shook my hand, nodded and pointed to Lou Borucki, the other intern assigned to her for our rotation on 8A—residents typically supervised two interns, each ideally responsible for eight to ten patients. Lou and I had met the night before on the roof of County Hospital and had figured out that we were both assigned to Dr. Weaver.

"Okay, John—Lou and I are going to round on his patients. I want you to get up to snuff on the two patients admitted last night—especially the young girl, Jeanie Perkins, who has lupus and a fever. She's very sick and needs immediate attention. Go see her and report back to me."

Jeanie Perkins—the name sounded familiar. Then it hit me: she was the wonderful young girl I met during the summer I had spent with Dr. Goldman two years previously. She was fourteen back then—smart, interested, pretty, full of life. She suffered from lupus, an autoimmune disorder in which the immune system attacks the patient's own tissues and organs. The clinical presentation can be highly variable depending on which systems are involved. It is often most severe in young females. I checked on her room number and hurried down the hall to find her. Now here she was, her rosy cheeks heightened by fever and the malar rash characteristic of lupus.

"Hi, John—I mean Doctor Fitchen—so we meet again," she said, flashing her winsome smile, now free of braces. She had that same engaging way about her. I asked her what had happened that had brought her to the hospital. She told me she'd had a little cold for the past week—runny nose, dry cough, and a low-grade fever. Then she'd developed a severe headache (posterior, bilateral), and a fever spiking as high as 105. Then, in the middle of the night she had become confused and disoriented, and her parents had brought her to the emergency room.

She said her parents had gone down to the cafeteria to get something to eat and should be back any minute. I did a quick neurologic exam—mental status, cranial nerves, muscle strength, reflexes—nothing remarkable. At least for the moment, she was oriented to time, place, and person—she knew the date, the day of the week, the location of her room, and the president (Nixon). As I was running through this examination, her parents appeared, looking worried and distressed. We ran through the events of the last couple of days. All they could add was that Jeanie had noted black stools the past two days—she had probably been too embarrassed to mention that to me.

Then—WHAM! Her arms and legs stiffened and began to shake, and her eyes rolled up—she was having a grand mal seizure. Struggling to stay calm, I tilted her head back to open her airway and told her father to find the nurse and tell her we needed Dr. Weaver right now. The seizure lasted about two minutes. It felt like two hours—but at last, Dr. Weaver and the nurse arrived. When it was over, Jeanie blinked her eyes and looked around at the people surrounding her bed. "What happened?" she asked.

"You've had a seizure," Dr. Weaver told her, "but it's OK now. We're going to give you medicine in your vein that will keep you from having another. I'm going to page Neurology and ask them for an emergency consult. John, stay here and start an IV, stat. Let me know immediately if there are any further neurological events." And she was gone. I took a deep breath, asked the nurse to bring me an IV tray, and told Jeanie and her parents to brace themselves for a lot of activity.

There was, indeed, to be a lot of activity. Over the next thirty-nine hours, as her heightened, self-destructive immune system attacked her own tissues, Jeanie's organs began to fail, one after the other. Her own immune cells and antibodies were causing inflammation and damage everywhere: brain (cerebritis), heart (pericarditis), lungs (bronchitis), kidneys (nephritis), stomach and bowels (gastroenteritis), and bone marrow (thrombocytopenia—low platelets—secondary to hematopoietic dysfunction). Nothing was spared.

Over the course of the day and evening she would be seen by eight consultants, each with a different take on what was happening and how it should be managed. Part of the trouble was that interventions recommended by one group of consultants would cause other consultants to warn of life-threatening complications. For example, several experts (especially the rheumatologists) recommended prednisone, a potent corticosteroid, but the infectious disease specialists feared that this might lead to serious, even fatal, systemic infection, and the endocrinologists cautioned that prednisone could induce severe diabetes. After careful deliberation, we decided to try it. I started Jeanie's IV—hard to believe my hands were steady given how shaky I felt inside.

Meanwhile, reality continued. I made rounds with Dr. Weaver, did the liver biopsy at one in the afternoon, met with consultant after consultant, and eventually worked up the two elective admissions (both of whom I had to awaken after midnight to complete a history and physical examination). To say that I "did" the liver biopsy is a stretch. Dr. Weaver literally held my hands through the whole procedure, standing behind me for good movement control, and pushing and pulling on my elbow at the critical moment when the biopsy needle was thrust in and out of the liver. The key was to have the patient hold his breath with lungs fully expanded. If he gasped as the needle was pushed in and out of the organ, he would be unable to breathe in further, and cause hepatic movement and the attendant risk of laceration.

But without question, my focus was on Jeanie. Throughout the day and continuing into and through the night, I spent hour after hour with the parade of consultants, and more time tracking down lab results, x-rays, and blood cultures. Despite all the activity, Jeanie was getting worse. Most alarming was her mental status. She was barely responsive. In addition, her platelets had dropped to 20,000 (very low), her blood urea nitrogen was rising—an indication of progressive kidney failure—prompting the nephrologists to recommend dialysis, there was blood in her stool (probably from gastritis combined with low platelets), and she had developed an abnormal heart rhythm.

Finally, around five in the evening on the second day of my internship, there was a quiet moment in the doctors' office with Dr. Weaver. I updated her on Jeanie's condition—not good—and told her that I had met with eight consultants, and that there were as many opinions as there were experts. Bottom line: Jeanie was dying and we had to do something.

"John," she said, "there comes a time when discussions and recommendations must come to an end—a time for action. You know more about Jeanie Perkins than any other doctor, including me. You have virtually lived at her bedside for the last day and a half. What do *you* think we should do? It's your call."

"I may know more about the patient, but you know more about the disease," I told her. "In any case, I think her chances are slim to none. Things just keep getting worse. As we discussed earlier, a couple of our consultants have mentioned mega-dose steroids, dexamethasone. If you give enough, it's supposed to rein in the immune system—and it's her immune system that's killing her. I know this may worsen her bleeding, I know she may get an overwhelming infection, I know she may die. But the way I see it, this is her only chance. And we should know in a couple of hours if it's going to help."

"Okay," she said, "then that's the plan. Will you talk it over with her parents? I'll come along if you like, but you do the talking."

We walked somberly to the room. Jeanie was now fully comatose, as she had been for several hours. Her mother was in the bed, cradling her daughter. Her dad tried to sleep in a bedside chair. Seeing me and Dr. Weaver enter the room, they became immediately alert. I gave them a synopsis of what had happened in the past several hours. It was essentially a picture of multi-organ failure. The situation was dire. I told them about dexamethasone and how, at very high doses, it could turn off the immune system—but that there was not much experience with the drug in this kind of circumstance, and that very serious, even fatal, side effects could occur. The risks were extreme. Without hesitation, they said they wanted to try it. They knew the odds were against us, and that this was the only hope. I was their doctor, and they would go with my advice.

I got the dexamethasone infusion right away from the pharmacy and, with the nurse, started the drip. Kathy asked to see me in the doctors' office. "John," she said. "You haven't slept for hours and hours. Take a break, get some rest. There is, you know, an on-call sleeping quarters. I've got things covered for the next couple of hours."

"I'm going to hang in," I replied. "I want to see if there's any response to the dexamethasone."

I returned to Jeanie's room, where the only illumination came from a couple of night-lights. I sat down next to the bed, held Jeanie's hand, and spoke quietly with her parents about what a wonderful kid their daughter was. We all eventually fell asleep. At about eight in the evening, we awakened as if on some collective cue. There was complete silence.

Jeanie was dead—cold skin, pupils fixed and dilated, no point in attempting CPR. She looked peaceful in the muted light.

I looked at her parents and started to cry, sobbing as

I told them how sorry I was, how hopeless and defeated I felt. They cried, too, trying through their tears to comfort me. They knew how hard I had tried, how much I hated losing this battle, how deeply I cared about their daughter.

I trudged home to our modest one-bedroom apartment a block and a half from the hospital, and folded into Ellen's arms. I was utterly drained, too beat to tell her the story, completely humbled, and too tired to eat more than a couple of bites of the meal she had prepared and held for hours. I flopped onto the bed and immediately fell asleep. It was midnight.

I will never forget the first thirty-nine hours of my internship. I was in awe of the power of pathology, the inadequacy of the medical arsenal. I wondered if we ever won.

But of course we did win—often quietly and incrementally, but sometimes dramatically. Take, for example, the stunning case of Mr. Carson, a sixty-two-year-old man with severe chronic obstructive pulmonary disease (COPD) who was admitted to the County Hospital MICU (Medical Intensive Care Unit) at the end of my internship. He presented with severe dyspnea (difficulty breathing), which was secondary to (caused by) acute bacterial bronchitis superimposed on his COPD. We gave him antibiotics and nasal oxygen, but eventually his oxygen level became dangerously low and we had to place an endotracheal tube (a tube inserted through the mouth or nose and into the windpipe) and attach it to a respirator. This proved to be of marginal help because we couldn't get him to "cooperate" with the machine—when it would breathe in, he would breathe out, and when it would breathe out, he would breathe in. We tried repeatedly to sedate him, but he continued to fight the respirator. He was fatiguing rapidly.

At 8:00 a.m. sharp, Donald G. Kassebaum, MD, our attending physician—known to all as "Kass," though we never called him that to his face—strode into the Unit and sized up the situation. He went straight to Mr. Carson. In crisp Teutonic tones, he hissed at us. "Why is this man thrashing about?" he demanded. The resident and I stiffened.

"Well, gee, Dr. Kassebaum, we've been giving him valium and morphine every hour, but we just can't seem to get him to cooperate with the ventilator," we replied.

"D-tubocurarine, twenty-four milligrams, stat," he intoned to the nurse. The resident and I stared silently at each other, hoping to avoid eye contact with Dr. Kassebaum. Had we heard him correctly? Was he actually going to give our patient a potentially fatal poison (curare), a neuromuscular alkaloid that would paralyze all his muscles, especially the ones with which he breathed?

The nurse returned, holding the syringe in front of her. So quickly had she left and returned, it seemed like the syringe was smoking. "Give him six milligrams," Kass instructed the nurse, and then waited about ten seconds. "Give him six more." Another brief wait, then "Give him six more," and then the final six. All of a sudden, everything kicked in—the valium, the morphine, the curare. The ventilator stopped bucking and settled into a quiet, steady rhythm. Before our eyes, the patient's color went from a sickly, ashen blue to pink. It was a miracle. Kass said not a word, allowing only a faint smile.

Of course, Dr. Kassebaum knew exactly what he was doing. Curare kills by paralyzing the respiratory muscles. But with the airway secured by the endotracheal tube and the machine doing the breathing, the lungs were now getting a steady flow of 100% oxygen and the patient was sleeping peacefully, buying time to let the antibiotics clear his bronchitis. It was an awesome display of knowledge and audacity. It saved a life.

By three that afternoon, Mr. Carson had been extubated and was asking for food and water. Two hours later he was well enough to be transferred out of the Unit and back to the ward. "Now *that*," said the resident, "is how a visit to the MICU is supposed to go down."

Internship was an extraordinary experience. I learned more in that one year than I had in the four years of med school that came before it. True, I was taught a new language during those years—I thought of it as becoming bilingual in English and medicine. But nothing compared to the depth and breadth of hands-on clinical experience crammed into that single riveting year. Most especially, I had learned the importance of knowing when you don't know—and of admitting it. Now I was a resident—not yet polished, but sufficiently trained to be able to supervise interns and students, and ready to grow with experience.

My first rotation as a resident was at Good Samaritan, an affiliated private hospital in northwest Portland. I was assigned to a general medicine ward similar to 8A at University Hospital. My first night on call, I was notified by the hospital operator that I was needed immediately in the Obstetrics suite.

"Are you sure you've got the right doctor?" I asked her. "I'm a medicine resident."

"Well, we double-checked the coverage chart and your name came up," she replied. "The private attending physician is on his way but won't be there for at least half an hour. The OB resident is doing a C-section with the obstetrician on call. Both surgical residents are in the OR with a trauma patient, and that leaves you, Dr. Fitchen. I'm just following protocol."

"Well … okay," I said. "But how do I get there? Where's the delivery room?"

I'd never been there. She gave me directions and I hustled off, wondering what would come my way, and trying to remember what I had done when I had delivered a baby, under close supervision, as a third-year medical student. I raced through the hospital and up four flights of stairs, then turned into the OB suite and peered down the hall.

A clutch of nurses was gathered outside the door to one of the delivery rooms at the far end of the hall—never a good sign. I plowed through and into the room. I ripped off my stethoscope and tossed it (inadvertently) onto a tray of sterilized instruments, and then managed to stick my thumb into the little finger end of the sterile gloves held out by the nurse. To hell with the gloves: the operative field wasn't sterile and we had to get moving. The top of the baby's head—the caput—was plainly visible, and I could see that the cervix was fully dilated and effaced. This baby was ready but had stalled. I introduced myself to the patient and placed a hand gently on her belly. "It's been a while since I did one of these," I told her, "but we'll work through it together."

The OB head nurse told me there had been no progress in the past half hour and she was concerned because the baby's heart rate was intermittently decelerating. "Have you thought about doing an episiotomy?" she asked.

"Right, sounds like a good idea," I replied. Without a word, she placed a pair of surgical scissors in my bare hand and indicated with her finger where the cut should be made. A couple of snips and the head began to come out. Dropping the scissors, I managed with both hands to control the delivery of the head and move it gradually through the birth canal. And then it was out! The baby filled the room with its cries. I was so relieved that I forgot there was more to come. As I released my grip, everything else—shoulders, buttocks, legs, placenta—flopped into my lap, covered with blood and other juices.

I told the patient she had a beautiful baby girl: pink, active, all ten fingers and all ten toes. She thanked me with great warmth and sincerity and told me I'd done a wonderful job. She said it seemed like I must do this all the time. "Very much a team effort," I told her, bowing to the head nurse and looking her in the eye. The nurses in the hallway were all clapping and shouting, "It's a girl, it's a girl!"

Just then the private obstetrician arrived, none too pleased that he had to clean up the mess and sew up the episiotomy while I got all the glory. I thanked the head nurse again for walking me through it. She shook my hand and gave me a knowing smile. "You did a fine job, doctor."

I bounded back to the on-call room and, even though it was two in the morning, called Ellen. Through tears of joy I told her what had happened. "I delivered a baby!" She loved it, and she loved me.

FIELD NOTES

A small- to medium-sized shorebird seen on the Columbia River about a mile east of Broughton Beach on 9/12/13. Overall pale with pure white underparts. Fast, smooth, and skilled at running on the sand at water's edge. Straight, thickish black bill. Black legs. Spangled back with black, gray, and white markings, no rufous coloration. Orange/tawny epaulets and faint wash on face. Black primaries seen at tip of tail.

Returned today (9/13/13) to check out likely habitat downstream from yesterday's sighting, and saw four or five additional birds. I saw the birds in flight and they have a fully black leading edge on the underwing and a broad white wing patch the length of the wing. Much better views of the backs of the birds—I was virtually looking straight down on them—which were boldly marked with black, white, and gray, and no rufous edging.

Bird #289.
Sanderling

[Code-4]

CHAPTER 11
USAFSAM

When I had graduated from medical school in 1971, the Vietnam War and its attendant draft were in full swing. As part of the so-called "doctor draft," medical students (who had been deferred through med school) were certain to be called to service upon graduation and completion of a year of post-MD clinical training (internship). In an effort to deliver more fully trained physicians to the military, an alternative was offered to graduating MDs under a program called the Berry Plan. If you chose to participate in the plan, you were given a second deferral while completing an additional year or two of specialty training (residency).

This seemed like a no-brainer to me. The longer I was deferred, the better the chances the war would end and I wouldn't have to face combat in Southeast Asia. After researching the possibilities, I decided to join the air force as a flight surgeon through the Berry Plan after a one-year deferral during which I completed my first year of residency in Portland. I chose the air force because it meant learning about aerospace medicine, and because I thought air force bases were located in cool places—a dubious notion, as I was to learn later.

When you joined the air force, you could go directly to your assigned base as a general medical officer (GMO), or you could add a few months to the standard two-year tour of duty and complete special training in aerospace medicine to become a flight surgeon. GMOs provided healthcare to ground personnel, flight surgeons provided care to flight personnel (pilots, navigators, flight engineers, and loadmasters). Training in aerospace medicine was carried out in a nine-week program at Brooks Air Force Base in San Antonio, Texas. The United States Air Force School of Aerospace Medicine (USAFSAM) facility had been dedicated by President Kennedy on November 21, 1963, the day before he was assassinated in Dallas. The dedication was his last official act as president.

Upon successful completion of the USAFSAM program, you were given the rank of captain, flight surgeon wings, and the title of "flight surgeon." Being a flight surgeon doesn't mean you perform surgery in airplanes—it means you are aware of the unique issues pertinent to the flight environment. For example, anyone would know that a pilot who breaks his leg needs to be grounded, but until you have watched a pilot crank down on the rudder pedal while landing a fully loaded C-141 cargo plane in a twenty-five-knot crosswind, you can't judge when he's ready to *return* to unrestricted flight status. The only way to understand the force required to perform this maneuver is if you have been there, in the cockpit, on top of the action, at close range.

Forty-seven of us reported to Brooks on October 3, 1973. We were almost uniformly out of shape, coming off two or three years of medical training and its hundred-hour workweeks. Despite our woeful physical condition, we were excited. We had this romantic notion that we were reporting to boot camp, ready to crawl through mud on our bellies, live machine gun bullets zipping over our heads.

This idea was debunked as soon as we arrived. Immediately after signing in, we were given $400 in cash to "tide us over," and the first week of class was devoted to grooming (no beards, mustaches permitted but not beyond the corners of the mouth, hair off the ears), saluting (how to do it, to whom to do it, and when to do it), and clothing (standard uniform, flight suit, fatigues, and mess dress). There was much discussion about the mess dress—it was expensive ($75) and likely never to be worn. But what if some special event came up and mess dress was mandatory? I ended up buying an ill-fitting used set for $30 and never wore it.

At the beginning of week two, we finally got some action. We were ordered to report to the airfield for PLFs (parachute-landing falls). On a knoll overlooking the runway—a site chosen, I reckon, to lend a certain authenticity to the exercise—was a looming tower. It had to be at least twenty feet high (gulp). Then we noticed a series of modest wooden platforms, ranging from one foot to four feet in height. The tower, we would later learn, would be used in subsequent jumping exercises that simulated the harnessed jolt experienced upon parachute opening. Today, our activities would be restricted to the small platforms.

Tech Sergeant Pratt was in charge. He explained that while flight surgeons were not being trained to parachute *out* of airplanes, we were being trained to fly *in* airplanes so we could observe flight personnel at work, and might encounter situations when we had to jump out of airplanes. ("Eject! Eject! Eject!") And if we did, we needed to know how to land. We were instructed to climb onto the platforms, starting with the one-footer. We were to stand sideways at the edge, stare at the horizon, hop off the side with knees partially bent, and upon impact with the ground, roll to the side to absorb the blow with quads and flank.

The impact was hardly noticeable at first, but as the height was increased, the ground came at us rather quickly. Sergeant Pratt didn't care so much about how we dropped, he cared about how we landed. We did it over and over, inching up to the four-foot platform for a final round of ten reps. The next morning, back at the classroom, we moved slowly and cautiously, creeping down the aisles with knees locked for fear of collapsing should we bend them even slightly—shades of locked knees after squat-thrusts in President Kennedy's high school fitness program.

I'm happy to report I never had to jump out of an airplane.

One section of the flight surgeon curriculum was devoted

to barometric pressure, and the consequences of too much or too little air—especially too little. A series of lectures on the topic was given by Lt. Col. "Chick" Prendergast, an old-school hard-assed instructor who kept us attentive by lacing his sentences with one expletive after another. We kept track. With apologies to the faint of heart, recounted here is an excerpt of his most expletive-suffused presentation, a forty-five-minute lecture on hypoxia:

> One day you fucking boys will run into some fucking cocksucker who thinks he's a smart fucking son-of-a-bitch and says he knows more about hypoxia than you motherfuckers ever would. You tell this shithead you were trained by "Chick" Prendergast, a fucking font of information, more fucking knowledge than any other fucking motherfucker in the world.

By the time he was done, we'd counted two hundred seventy-three "fucks" and variations thereof ("fuck, fucking, fucker, motherfucker"—about one every ten seconds), and "shits," "bitches," and "damns" too numerous to count.

We listened carefully and remembered his words of wisdom when we participated in a subsequent rapid decompression drill. We were ushered into a special hypoxia chamber capable of taking ambient pressure from sea level to 25,000 feet in less than two seconds. That's roughly equivalent to climbing from New Delhi (elevation 820 feet) to the South Col on Mount Everest (elevation 25,938 feet) in two blinks of an eye. We were seated on benches with folding desks and given paper and pencil. We were told to sign our names, over and over, down the page. If we felt any impairment, we were to raise our hand

and an instructor equipped with oxygen masks would tend to us immediately.

The instructors looked in the eyes of every participant, we all gave a thumbs-up, we started signing our names, and someone on the outside flipped a switch. There was a sudden loud "clap," then silence as the chamber turned foggy. A few minutes into the drill, two of the students slumped onto their desks and were instantly fitted with oxygen masks. Neither they nor anyone else still conscious raised a hand. The drill was soon concluded and pressure restored. We were asked by the instructors not to look at our signature page and to share our thoughts on the quality of our penmanship. To a man, we said it was fine, excellent in fact. Then we were asked to look down. What had started as orderly, legible signatures deteriorated into essentially straight lines—perhaps "flat lines" is a more appropriate term.

In the discussion that followed the exercise, the recurring theme was the insidious nature of hypoxia: we didn't just perform poorly, we had no idea we had performed poorly—*nobody had raised a hand*. It was interesting to note that during the hypoxia conversation, Colonel Prendergast said almost nary a swear word. The topic was compelling in its own right, without need of embellishment. Pilots died for failure to recognize hypoxia and its treacherous effects.

At the end of Colonel Prendergast's teaching segment there was some extra time which he used to ask us about our specific base assignments—an impressive array of places across the nation and around the world, with special focus on Southeast Asia. If you were unmarried, you were likely to be assigned to a base in or near Vietnam; if you were married, you were likely to be assigned stateside (thank you, Ellen). This was all routine fare for the colonel until one kid indicated that he was headed to Minot AFB in North Dakota, home to strategic bomber and missile wings. The colonel paused, pondered, and whispered loudly to the kid in his southern drawl, "Motherfucker, you gonna be SACified"—alluding to the high-security, high-tension environment associated with nuclear weapons, and operations carried out at SAC (Strategic Air Command) bases like Minot.

I was not SACified. I was assigned to Norton AFB in San Bernardino, CA. At the time, Norton was part of the Military Airlift Command. It housed the 63d Military Airlift Wing with two squadrons of C-141 Starlifter cargo aircraft. San Bernardino was not exactly a glamorous assignment. As near as I could tell, its only claims to fame were that it was home to the founding chapter of the Hells Angels Motorcycle Club and the site of the first McDonald's hamburger stand.

The base medical facility was modest—four flight surgeons, six GMOs, a tiny emergency room, and minimal but excellent support staff. Much of what we did in the flight clinic was pretty boring, mostly annual check-ups for healthy young flight personnel. We organized our activities anatomically from top to bottom—that is, eyes and ears (especially eyes—pilots have very high standards for visual acuity), hearts and lungs (you could get grounded for an innocent heart murmur or modest elevation of blood pressure), and "nuts and butts" (palpation of the testicles to rule out testicular cancer, a relatively common tumor in young males, and digital rectal exam—the "finger wave," as it was called by the pilots; the latter was admittedly of marginal screening value in healthy young men, but it got their attention).

One day, Tech Sgt. Wesley Jones ("Jonesie") came to my office to tell me we had a problem. A full-bull colonel was in for his annual physical and was throwing his elbows around—cutting into line and disrupting the flow. I walked out to the reception area and saw immediately that Jonesie's report was accurate. The colonel was railing at the staff about how busy and important he was. He didn't have time for a goddamn finger wave and had to get back to work right away.

"Howdy, Colonel," I said. "How's it going?"

"It's not going at all," he replied, looking closely at the margin of my mustache, clearly beyond the corners of my mouth. "What kind of sloppy outfit are you running here, Captain? Can't your staff provide some timely service? I need to get to the front of this fucking line and get the hell out of here."

"Now, Colonel, I don't like to see you getting all worked up about this. I'm worried you're gonna raise your blood pressure and then I'll have to ground you while we look into this. We'd need to send you up to Travis for a full cardiac evaluation. That could take months. Now why don't you just settle down and take your place in line like everybody else?"

He knew I had him by the balls. Essentially, I controlled his flight status. If his blood pressure was up, even a little (and, of course, I would want to check it myself), I could ground him and assign him to "duty not involving flying" (DNIF) and he would lose his flight pay, a hefty chunk for a high-ranking colonel. In the clinic, it mattered not that he outranked me by a lot. He needed my blessing, because without it he couldn't fly. He sighed deeply and plodded off to the back of the line.

Early in my tenure at Norton AFB, I was asked by one of the GMOs if he could see me for his discharge exam. I said sure and asked if he had any significant medical history. He told me he had been diagnosed with granulomatous ileocolitis (an inflammatory bowel disease) complicated by amyloidosis of the liver and kidneys (deposition of amyloid protein in these organs), but that he had improved dramatically after removal of the involved bowel—a very unusual approach. I blinked a few times, absorbed what he had just told me, and said, "That's an amazing story. Where can I read about you in the medical literature?" He said there was a nephrology fellow at the University of Washington who had talked about writing it up, but he had gone into private practice and dropped the project.

With the patient's permission, I contacted the UW Department of Pathology, who cooperatively sent me the relevant slides. I managed to track down a medical photographer who took pre- and post-surgery micrographs of the liver showing dramatic resolution of amyloid deposition. This was very rare and worthy of publication. Being the naïve young doctor that I was, I figured I'd write it up and send it off to the *New England Journal of Medicine*. I had no idea how difficult it is to publish an article, even a case

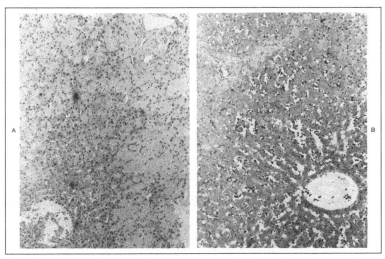

Liver biopsies at the time of bowel operation (*left*) showing extensive deposition of amyloid protein (light, homogeneous, acellular material) which compresses and replaces normal hepatic tissue; and one year after operation (*right*) showing marked reduction of amyloid deposition and return of normal liver architecture (image originally published in *New England Journal of Medicine*, JH Fitchen, "Amyloidosis and granulomatous ileocolitis: Regression after surgical removal of the involved bowel." 292(7):352-3, 1975. Copyright © Massachusetts Medical Society. Reprinted with permission)

report, in that prestigious journal. So I put it together, sent it off, and forgot about it. Six weeks later I received notification that they would publish my case report if I could cut it by 90 percent. I was shattered. How could I possibly cut so much? My purple prose down the drain. It was like murdering your children. But cut it I did, and publish it they did. My first publication: a single-author paper in the *NEJM*. It was starting to feel like academic medicine was the right choice for me.

As flight surgeons, we were required to fly regularly in order to remain current in flight medicine. This usually involved local and regional flying, but every few months we would participate in overseas missions. On these longer trips, we got a bird's-eye view of the effects of time-zone changes and jet lag.

One particularly memorable excursion entailed the delivery of ten pallets of toilet paper to the US space tracking station in Alice Springs, Australia. We were alerted at 0100 (1:00 a.m.) for an 0400 departure. We grabbed a little breakfast before departure, and I, wanting to keep track of my expenditures, entered carefully in my notebook, "0300: Breakfast." We left on time and flew north to Travis AFB outside Sacramento. While the pallets of TP were being loaded, we grabbed a bite to eat, and I entered "0600: Breakfast" in my notebook.

The next leg took us from Travis to Hickam in Honolulu. We arrived at 1000 and, after beer call, settled into a hearty meal of scrambled eggs and sausage, and I entered, "1100: Breakfast" in my notebook. We slept for four or five hours before being alerted at 1900 for a 2000 departure. In an effort to maximize sleep, we had left no time for food. However, while the aircraft was being refueled in Pago Pago there was time for a quick meal; I entered in my notebook, "0700: Breakfast" before we took off on the leg to New Zealand. As we began our approach into Christchurch, the pilot activated the intercom.

"Okay, cockpit, listen up," he said. "We've flown a lot of miles and haven't had a lot of sleep. We've crossed seven time zones, the International Dateline, the equator, and we're all a little punchy. So everyone closely monitor ATC radio traffic." ATC was air traffic control.

I was sitting in the jump seat, situated between the pilot and co-pilot, and had a perfect view of the relevant instruments. No sooner had the pilot completed his instructions than the radio crackled to life. "MAC5021niner, Christchurch. Descend and maintain 11—one-one—thousand feet, reduce airspeed to 250 knots, and turn left to heading 260 degrees."

I watched the altimeter, the airspeed indicator, and the compass as we descended and slowed and turned. As we neared 11,000 feet, the pilot slowed the rate of descent until we reached and held the designated altitude. The heading was another matter. As we turned left, the compass showed 290, 280, 270, 260 … 250 (!). Noticing that we'd passed the designated 260 degrees, I poked the pilot in the shoulder and shouted at him over the engine noise, "Check your heading!" He looked at me, rolled his eyes at his mistake, and corrected the heading.

I was (and am) in awe of what pilots do. Any one of the maneuvers required for positioning and landing a 340,000-pound, four-engine jet airplane is challenging—but to execute multiple simultaneous maneuvers, especially reducing speed while losing altitude, requires exceptional talent, training, and focus.

The heading glitch behind us, we landed without incident—a real "greaser," so smooth you had to look out the window to see if we were on the ground. That night we had a much-needed period of crew rest (sixteen hours) and wonderful New Zealand steaks. Finally, I could write in my notebook, "1900: *Dinner.*"

The next morning we saddled up for the flight to Alice Springs to deliver our precious cargo. Alice Springs, a tiny dot on the map, is in the middle of the outback.

We happened to arrive at the height of a major hatching of bush flies. There was nowhere to hide—wherever we turned there were waves of them, crawling down our necks, buzzing in our ears. We endeavored to get some food, but the flies were as thick inside the restaurant as outside, and swarmed all over our soggy hotdogs. The locals seemed barely to notice the relentless onslaught. They were just glad to have restored their stock of toilet paper. Finally, the off-loading was completed and we returned to the C-141. We wasted no time in taking off and heading for Sydney, where we would luxuriate in a full forty-eight hours of crew rest.

At last we were able to settle in and stay put—no time zones to cross, no pressure to move on. We stayed in King's Cross, the epicenter of Sydney nightlife. The natives were warm and friendly, the sightseeing magnificent. We slept, we ate, we sunned, we drank too much, we communed with the locals.

At three in the morning on the second night, there was a frantic pounding on my door. One of my comrades beseeched me to give him "emergency antibiotics." Too tired to argue, I gave him a couple of tetracycline capsules (from a stash provided to me before departing Norton by a fellow flight surgeon—"just in case"), and told him to get some sleep and check back with me in the morning. The next day he was fine—no drip, no burning, no problem. After two days and nights of partying in the wee hours, we needed some sleep. The tongue-in-cheek wisdom was that we needed to get back on the airplane to get some rest.

Ready to move on after our forty-eight hours in Sydney, we reported for duty and headed for home. The trip was smooth except for a couple of events that were out of the ordinary, at least for me. We were cruising along on autopilot at 37,000 feet when the pilots, looking for some action, asked if I'd like to have a stab at delivering air reports. These reports were radioed from aircraft flying across the Pacific Ocean to ground stations such as the one at Hickam. By gathering this information from hundreds of aircraft, the Weather Service could piece together valuable data points to describe the global weather picture. The pilots gave me a form containing a sequence of about thirty numbers. I was to call up Hickam AFB on the radio and read off these numbers in precise order. The numbers could be transformed at the other end into meaningful information about weather conditions at a certain altitude over the ocean. With the pilots looking on, I initiated the sequence.

"Hickam, Hickam; MAC 5021niner with AirRep," I said into the microphone.

"Roger, 21niner, you are loud and clear," came the almost instant reply.

I then rattled off the sequence of numbers in the best baritone I could muster, and finished off with "Maintenance status is Alpha-One," indicating that we had no indications of equipment malfunction that would need attention at Hickam. The pilots nodded their approval.

"Nice job, Doc. Now how about flying this beast? Want to give it a try?"

After all the hours of flying on autopilot, they apparently thought this would be "good for laughs." I wasn't so sure this was a good idea, but I realized we were 37,000 feet above the ocean and thousands of miles from any appreciable landmass, so there wasn't much that could go wrong. Without further deliberation, the pilot shifted to the jump seat and I climbed into the left seat and strapped into my seatbelt.

Once I was adjusted and settled, the pilot told me to "grasp the yoke but don't do anything else until I tell you. Now you'll notice that your right hand is just above a button on the yoke. When I give the nod, I want you to push that button with your right thumb and then don't do anything."

He nodded, and I pushed.

"Your airplane, Doctor."

There was a little jolt and then nothing—smooth sailing. The button had turned off the autopilot, and I was flying a C-141. Or maybe I should say it was flying me. I wish I could report that I was calm, cool, and collected—but alas, I wasn't. I gripped the yoke with white knuckles and tried not to flinch.

"How about a step climb?" the pilot asked.

"Okay—what do I do?" I said, my voice cracking at the end.

"Give it a little throttle and pull back gently on the yoke. Keep your eye on the altimeter, and when we hit flight level 390"—meaning 39,000 feet—"pull back on the throttle and push gently forward on the yoke."

I did as instructed, and then, after five minutes at the new altitude, reversed the process. As we settled back down to flight level 370, I heaved a sigh of relief. So far, so good.

"Wanna try a turn?" the pilot asked. I thought this over for all of two seconds before telling him, "You know, I think maybe we should quit while we're ahead. Thanks for letting me fly your airplane."

This photo was a gift from my nephew, Chris Fitchen, a T-38 flight instructor; he photoshopped my head onto his body

He smiled as he replied, "Doc, I'll fly with you anytime, anywhere."

Overly generous of this fine young man, but it felt mighty good. And the rest of the way home I couldn't stop grinning.

FIELD NOTES

A group of shorebirds found on Smith Lake across from Blind A near the end of the large peninsula on 9/17/13. Quite distant and near the limits of the optics, especially when thermals were in play, but the dramatic upturned bill was distinctive. A large, long-legged shorebird, it uses its upturned bill as a scythe, whipping horizontally from side to side in the mud. White birds overall, with black wings and white central scapulars on perched bird. Black distal feathers on bird in flight. Leg color not detected at this distance, but clearly long-legged. Joined by Art Clausing and Tait Anderson, who concurred with the diagnosis.

Bird #290.
American Avocet
[Code-4]

CHAPTER 12

RE-ENTRY, FELLOWSHIP, AND MY FIRST LIFE BIRD

In the fall of 1975, when I finished my tour of duty as a flight surgeon at Norton AFB, I returned to Oregon to complete my medical residency. My first assignment was a four-week rotation on the neurology ward. I knew little about this discipline—a situation aggravated by two years away from critical care medicine. I was thirty.

At eight in the morning on the first day, I walked down the hall to the doctors' office and introduced myself to the neurology resident. I told him I was just back from a two-year stint in the air force and was accordingly a little out of touch, medically. He gave me a quick run-down of the activities of the night before: three admissions—a seventy-five-year-old man with a first-time thromboembolic stroke; a twenty-nine-year-old woman with an exacerbation of multiple sclerosis;

and a forty-six-year-old woman in an unexplained coma. He told me he had sent the coma patient off for a CAT scan, the results of which should be ready in time for rounds with Dr. Hammerstad at nine.

"CAT scan?" I asked. "What's that?"

"Wow, you *are* out of touch. CAT: Computerized Axial Tomography, a glorified, high-resolution form of x-ray that can provide precise images of the brain and other tissues and organs."

I was embarrassed. After a mere two years in the air force, I was woefully out of date. Granted, I had been assigned to a low-level, low-tech outpatient facility, but it was stunning how fast medicine had progressed during my relatively brief absence.

"Bear with me," I said to the resident. "I'll get with the program."

Dr. John Hammerstad arrived at nine o'clock sharp and, reinforced by two third-year medical students and a registered nurse, our little entourage of six (including me and the neurology resident) set forth on rounds. The first patient we came to was the comatose woman. She remained unresponsive. The resident had received the CAT scan results—no intracranial masses, no hemorrhage, no inflammation, and the standard EEG (electroencephalogram) was normal.

"Did they do a nasopharyngeal lead?" asked Dr. Hammerstad.

"Uh, no sir, why would they?" asked the neurology resident. Dr. Hammerstad glared briefly at the resident, and then leaned down, studying at very close range the patient's eyelids. He looked at the group.

"Anybody see what I do? Does anything seem peculiar

about the eyelids? Nurse, please bring me a syringe with twenty milligrams of Valium for IV injection. And while she's preparing that, I want each of you to look very closely at the patient's eyelids." We did as instructed, and noticed, sort of, a slight flickering of the upper lids.

"Okay," he told us, "stand back!" As we stood around the bed, he gave the intravenous Valium (all twenty milligrams of it at once—*four times* the usual oral dose of five milligrams, and straight into the vein). Within seconds, the patient blinked, stared wide-eyed at the six of us looking down at her. She sat bolt upright in the bed and said, "Where am I?"

We were dumbfounded. The patient had received a prodigious intravenous dose of a potent sedative, enough to put the rest of us instantly to sleep, and she *woke up!*

Dr. Hammerstad was clearly pleased, in his quiet and wonderful way. He took the patient's hand gently in his own, told her she was at University Hospital, that she had been in a coma for nearly twenty-four hours, but that she was now awake and back to normal. He asked if this had ever happened before. It hadn't. He asked if there was anything that would make her more comfortable. "A ham and cheese sandwich," she said.

As Dr. Hammerstad later explained, the woman had a form of epilepsy called petit mal (literally "small bad") that involves small muscle groups—not the large muscle groups that twitch in grand mal ("large bad") seizures. Our patient was in a coma because she had status petit mal—"status," as in static, or continuous. A small area in her forebrain was continually firing, causing the eyelids to quiver and her cognition to be suppressed. The Valium had halted the twitching of the neurons and allowed her to awaken. After a day of observation on low-dose oral Valium, she was discharged for outpatient follow-up.

Over the ensuing months, as I completed rotations at County Hospital, Good Samaritan, University Hospital, and the VA, I felt progressively more confident and up-to-date, eventually hitting my full stride. But I realized I couldn't be a resident forever. My future awaited me and I needed to make some decisions. After three years of residency in internal medicine, I could go directly into private practice, or I could sign up for two or three years of additional training in a subspecialty (cardiology, nephrology, hematology, etc.) on a pathway either to subspecialty clinical practice or academic medicine.

Ultimately, the decision was forced when I was offered the position of Chief Resident, to be shared with Lou Borucki, a good man I'd met on the roof of County Hospital the night before internship started, and again on 8A at the beginning of our internship. Chief residency is a prestigious, high-profile post. In this role, one serves as the leader of the house staff, essentially organizing their educational experience. They plan, coordinate, and execute departmental conferences (e.g., morning report, grand rounds), rotational scheduling, and communications with subspecialty divisions.

I was honored by the suggestion that I might play that role, especially alongside Lou. But as I thought about the options, it was increasingly clear that I wanted to end up in academics, on the faculty of a major medical university.

While a chief residency would look good on my CV, the sooner I got into a subspecialty track, and into a strong program of teaching and research, the better off I would be.

The choice of subspecialty was relatively easy. The excitement I had felt at the two-headed microscope with Dr. Goldman in the summer of 1969 remained vivid seven years later, and it was clear that hematology / medical oncology was the flavor of medicine I wanted to pursue. Medical oncology was a fairly recently defined subspecialty that had grown out of hematology—in particular out of the diagnosis and treatment of patients with leukemia and lymphoma (the so-called "liquid" tumors). These patients were the first to be treated with chemotherapy. As success and experience accumulated with these disorders, chemotherapy was applied to patients with "solid" tumors (lung, colon, and others). At most medical centers, hematology and medical oncology, "heme-onc," encompassed the care and treatment of patients receiving chemotherapy.

The notion of proceeding to a heme-onc fellowship was reinforced by conversations with Dr. Grover Bagby, a high-powered heme-onc fellow at University Hospital, who told me the hottest program in the field was at UCLA. It offered a research focus on hematopoiesis (hemato = blood; poiesis = production), essentially the function of the bone marrow. The UCLA program was run by Dr. Martin J. Cline, who was internationally acclaimed for his seminal research in the field. I decided to apply and was invited for an interview.

In preparation for my interview with Dr. Cline, I spent a full weekend in the library reading and rereading scores of the scientific papers published by Cline and Dr. David Golde, his first lieutenant. Basically, Cline worked on granulopoiesis (white blood cell production), Golde worked on erythropoiesis (red cell production), and when indicated, they shared projects that involved both cell lineages of hematopoietic development.

The interview went well. They seemed impressed when I asked well-informed questions pertinent to the findings and conclusions I drew from their writings.

As part of the interview process, I accompanied Dr. Cline and his entourage on rounds. One patient had a markedly deformed thumbnail. I asked Dr. Cline what he made of the patient's onichogryposis.

"His what?" he said.

"Oh," I replied. "Onichogryposis. His right thumbnail has the typical ram's horn deformity."

Not missing a beat, and with a bit of a wink, he asked me if onichogryposis had anything to do with Zenker's degeneration of the stapedius muscle.

"Not to my knowledge," I replied, "but perhaps you could elaborate."

He did, though as near as I could tell, there was no connection. Suffice it to say that Dr. Cline and I were feeling good vibes. He seemed impressed, as well, that I had managed to get a single-author paper (albeit a case report) published in the *New England Journal of Medicine* while serving as a flight surgeon in the air force. (For context, nearly all scientific papers have multiple authors.) To my great delight, at the end of the day, he offered me a coveted heme-onc fellowship position in his program.

In July 1976, Ellen and I made the move from Portland to LA and I began my fellowship. Being part of a world-class medical research operation is a heady experience. There is a certain buzz, an excitement that pervades the environment, a feeling that everyday conversations could lead to important insights, new directions. Discovery is propelled by a combination of competition and collegiality.

There were seven of us first-year fellows who started that year. I had the good fortune of being assigned Dr. Cline as my research mentor. I told him I was interested in studying bone marrow failure. I realized that in order to understand why and how bone marrow fails, we must first understand how it functions normally—how it receives and transmits information through structures on the cell surface. This process involves growing marrow *in vitro* (a recently developed technique in which bone marrow cells could be grown in a petri dish, analogous to standard tissue culture) so as to control variables such as cell surface antigens that affect growth and differentiation of bone marrow progenitors, or stem cells. And in order to do that, we needed a source of normal human bone marrow. Given the hierarchy in the lab, with fellows at the bottom, *we* were the logical source of this marrow.

A graphical representation of this hierarchy was put together by "fellow fellow" Ken Foon. It was patterned after hematopoiesis, with Dr. Cline at the center—the pluripotent stem cell from which arose the rest of us in various stages of differentiation.

The standard procedure that we would perform on each other was bone marrow aspiration from the iliac (pelvic) bone. During my first year in the lab, I had thirty marrows performed on me. I know because we were paid

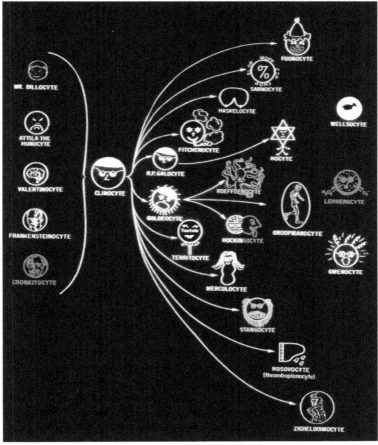

Pluripotent stem cell Cline (the "Clinocyte") is at the center of the UCLA Division of Hematology/Oncology; this tongue-in-cheek display of stages of differentiation was produced by Dr. Ken Foon

$70 per marrow, and over that time I declared $2,100 of earned income (earned, indeed!) from the procedures.

One of those stands out. It was performed on me by Dr. Cline. This was unusual—but for some reason all the fellows were occupied. And, alas, Dr. Cline was in a hurry. No time to talk or wait. He anesthetized the skin and then the periosteum (a highly sensitive tissue surrounding bones), but didn't wait for the anesthetic to have much effect. What was worse, he was unable to suck out any marrow on the first try (a so-called "dry tap"). Then, rather than pulling the needle out and starting over, he dragged the needle tip across the periosteum to another site. This movement was excruciatingly painful, but given my respect for Dr. Cline, I was darned if I was going to complain. I didn't make a peep.

Thank god the redraw was successful and a good sample obtained. And as a result of that experience, I'm sure I improved my bone marrow aspiration skills— namely, talk the patient through the process every step of the way, wait for the anesthetic to take full effect, and if there is a dry tap take the needle out and re-anesthetize the periosteum before proceeding.

My bone marrow experience notwithstanding, Dr. Cline was magnificent—an extraordinary mentor, an inspiring leader. He was simultaneously challenging and supportive, and a master at focusing himself or a discussion. He brought bright people together and stimulated discourse. When it was crunch time—that is, before a grant deadline—he would hole up in his office and hang a hotel "Do Not Disturb" sign on his doorknob. He meant it, and if you checked with his secretary to get a sense of how firm the message was today (sometimes he got absorbed and forgot the sign was hanging on his door), she would tell you without uttering a word—a nod yes, a shake no, or a "so-so" hand gesture warning you to proceed at your own risk.

But one day I just went and knocked on his door—no check-in with the secretary, no hesitation. I heard a great groan within the office and then a growled "What?" I opened the door and took the plunge. He didn't look pleased. In fact, he looked totally pissed.

"Our medical progress paper on the antigenic characteristics of hematopoietic stem cells has been accepted for publication in the *New England Journal of Medicine*," I blurted out. His demeanor softened noticeably.

"Way to go, John—that's terrific news. I want to hear all the details when this damn grant is out the door. Meanwhile, don't tell anyone you knocked while the sign was out. Talk to you soon."

A major focus of fellowship and academic medicine in particular was attending professional meetings. The big show was the annual meeting of the American Society of Hematology (ASH), held in December in a major US city. These meetings provided a forum for presentation (and criticism) of the latest scientific developments. They were often raucous and sometimes outright contentious. I recall one meeting where the speaker was asked a particularly venomous question in a shout from the audience. Then suddenly from the back of the room came the high-pitched voice of a five-year-old who jumped up on his chair and screamed, "You can't say that to him. He's my daddy!" The situation was immediately defused as the auditorium exploded in laughter.

Another masterful response was pulled off by Dr.

Golde. He was giving a high-pressure speech to the plenary session of the ASH annual meeting—a high honor. The room would not accommodate all of the attendees, so the audiovisual people had arranged a TV feed into a couple of adjacent anterooms. This required stronger lighting on the podium than was usual. At the end of his presentation, Golde received a mean-spirited, accusatory question from the audience. He squinted into the powerful lights and said, "The lights, the lights ... they're too bright, I can't hear. Next question please."

We also attended smaller-scale meetings, most notably in Keystone, Colorado. These scientific symposia were meant to bring together leading experts in focused topics such as hematopoiesis. They were sponsored by UCLA, and consisted of about a hundred participants. Because of the UCLA connection, many of us fellows were invited to go to Keystone. The schedule was wonderful: speeches from nine in the morning to noon, followed by a quick lunch. After that, we'd take a short bus ride to the ski area, where we'd enjoy run after run down gentle slopes with perfect snow. At four or five in the evening we'd head back to the lodge for wine and cheese. We'd have an informal dinner around six, and then reconvene for poster presentations from seven until ten. The informal atmosphere was conducive to impromptu discussions on the slopes and in the conference rooms.

A special treat at my first Keystone meeting was putting the faces together with the names. Most of the leading researchers in the field of hematopoiesis were there—names I associated with particularly important papers or fundamental discoveries. In my mind's eye I imagined them as giants, Greek gods who stood like statues, tall and fit. And then, there they would be: short, portly, balding; or tall, skinny, and bearded. But every one of them was smart, curious, tuned in. Most of all, they all seemed happy.

Perhaps the best scientific talk I have ever heard was at a Keystone meeting. It was presented by Drs. George Stamatoyannopoulos and Thalia Papayannopoulou, from the Fred Hutchinson Cancer Research Center at the University of Washington. They presented glorious fluorescent images of cell surface structures at various stages of hematopoietic differentiation: antigens, epitopes, potential targets of intercellular signaling. The work was beautiful, incontrovertible, scientifically and esthetically appealing. No nasty questions at the end of this one, just a very loud standing ovation—a rarity at Keystone meetings. To top it off, the word in the hallways was that George and Thalia were planning to get married. And when they did, the story went, they might hyphenate.

Though research was the primary focus of a fellowship intended to lead to a career in academic medicine, we also spent a substantial amount of time and effort on clinical activities. We did rotations on the heme-onc consult service and followed patients in the heme-onc clinic. One of my favorite patients was "Chip" Carmandola, a forty-two-year-old card-carrying member of the California Highway Patrol. He rode a Big Dog motorcycle and kept the peace. He had longstanding chronic lymphocytic leukemia more or less controlled with chlorambucil, an oral chemotherapy drug with modest side effects. As part of his leukemia, he had massive cervical adenopathy—enlarged lymph nodes in the neck. Each visit I would tell him that we could shrink those nodes with stronger medicine or a little low-dose radiation.

"No way!" he said. He told me that suspects didn't mess with him when they saw his big, thick neck. "Leave the neck alone, Doc."

In 1979, after three years of fellowship at UCLA, I was given an appointment as an assistant professor of medicine, with dedicated lab space and modest clinical responsibilities. I focused on securing funding and publishing papers—thirty in four-plus years at UCLA.

On January 17, 1981, there came a sudden call from Dr. Grover Bagby in Portland. His department had just received confirmation that they had secured funding for a new, hard-money, tenure-track position at the Portland VA, with an academic appointment at the med school. But I had to commit by January 20, because the moment he took office, the new president, Ronald Reagan, would impose an across-the-board hiring freeze on all federal appointments. Accordingly, Grover asked if Ellen and I could arrange to come up to Portland to interview; meet with him and Scott Goodnight, the acting division head; dine with George Porter, the chairman of the Department of Medicine, who insisted on standard protocol; and make a decision in three days.

I had had a wonderful run at UCLA and would forever feel an attachment to Dr. Cline, his people, and his program. But Ellen and I had loved Portland and were mightily tempted by the chance to return. I wouldn't have to start until July 1, but the decision had to be made before noon eastern standard time on January 20, when President Reagan was to be sworn in. The delayed start would give us some time to sell our house, which we had occupied for only two years, and to phase out gracefully at UCLA. But for now, we had to scramble to arrange care for our first child, Matthew, by then eighteen months old (thank you Grandma for the last-minute coverage); fly to Portland the morning of the eighteenth; interview with Scott and Grover and other members of the division; dine with Dr. and Mrs. Porter; and then reconvene with Scott after dinner. Scott said that my publication record was excellent, that I would fit in well, and that Dr. Porter was on-board. Scott offered me the job.

Ellen and I flew back to LA early the next morning and spent the whole day at the kitchen table listing and discussing the pros and cons of staying or moving. What ultimately swayed us to move was Matthew. We wanted to raise him—and hopefully another child—in a safe, family-oriented environment. This was LA, after all, and family life wasn't easy or actively supported. At the time, LA had suffered a spate of random shootings, and that gave us pause. We decided to move, and at the prearranged hour (eight in the morning, Pacific standard time—an hour to spare) I called Scott Goodnight and told him how pleased I was to accept the offer.

Before we left Los Angeles and returned to Portland, a quiet but momentous event occurred—I wrote down the name of a bird in a notebook. Dating back to childhood and nature walks with Dad, I had long been aware of birds, but had never before written down one's name.

We were sitting on our front porch on Ridgeley Drive, watching the world go by, when we became aware of a noisy bird calling from the treetops by the street. Its calls were loud, varied, with repeated musical phrases followed by a pause. We got some brief glimpses—enough to tell that the bird was gray overall, about the size of a robin, with a long tail and dramatic white wing patches when it flew—unequivocally a Northern Mockingbird.

I'm not sure why I wrote it down—and later checked it off on an American Birding Association checklist—but because I did, I figure this was my first of what turned out to be many "life birds" (a term birders use to designate their first identification of a species in the wild). In that defining moment, I had become a birder—a novice birder, but a birder nonetheless.

In the years that followed, my interest in birds grew steadily, and involved increasingly demanding travel and adventurous treks, culminating in a grand adventure to Attu, the western-most Aleutian island—recounted in chapter seventeen.

FIELD NOTES

A medium- to large-sized shorebird seen on 9/23/14, at the southwest end of Sturgeon Lake. Tough to ID because of heat waves, but overall size, shape, and coloration well seen. Unmarked breast and belly. Yellow-green legs. Scaly, buffy back. More bulky and buffy overall than associated Pectoral Sandpipers and yellowlegs.

Bird #291. **Ruff**

[Code-5]

CHAPTER 13

ACADEMIC MEDICINE

In its fullest expression, academic medicine is a high calling, a demanding profession comprised of teaching, research, and clinical activities. To do all these things well—to be a so-called "triple threat"—is a lofty goal much sought-after but rarely achieved. I had the good fortune of participating in all three, but never simultaneously—that was beyond my multitasking capacity. I loved doing each of them, perhaps especially teaching. They were all fun and challenging and engaging.

As luck would have it, the *New England Journal* medical progress paper I had written with Dr. Cline and my colleague Ken Foon at UCLA was published on July 2, 1981—my second day at work as an associate professor of medicine at the University of Oregon School of Medicine. Everywhere I went, it was all the buzz—a great way to start. But it came with pressure to live up to my own example.

That opportunity came sooner than I had anticipated. I was approached in August by the chief residents and invited to be the discussant in a Clinico-Pathologic Conference (CPC). An account of how these conferences were conducted and what I had to say is described in a letter I sent to my parents. Here's what I wrote them (edited for clarity):

Dear Mom and Dad,

I am currently nursing a wicked cold, no doubt precipitated by the onset of the rainy season together with unusually intense pressure to produce over the past six weeks. I seem to have turned the corner on the cold, and the spate of pressing priorities is finally under control.

The biggest sweat was my first CPC, which took place on September 18. The CPC is one of the time-honored trials by fire for young (and old) medical faculty. Well in advance (in my case, five weeks), one is given an account of the history, physical findings, and preliminary laboratory results from a particularly interesting and vexing case. At the end of this narrative it usually says something like "a diagnostic procedure was performed."

As the discussant, you are told neither what the procedure was nor what it revealed. Your task is to speak for forty to forty-five minutes on the differential diagnosis called to mind by the features of the case at hand, to adduce logical reasons for excluding most of these possibilities, and then to state what you believe the procedure was, what it revealed—and therefore, what the diagnosis was. After you have thus gone on record, a pathologist stands up and informs the audience of what, in fact, the procedure and the findings were. The chief resident told me beforehand that he couldn't believe there was any way I could get it right (*great*, I thought to myself).

The case with which I had to grapple was indeed perplexing: a twenty-three-year-old convict with an unusual vasculitic rash, weight loss, hepatospleno-megaly (enlarged liver and spleen), and dramatic eosinophilia (increase in eosinophils, a type of white blood cell characterized by bright red cytoplasm that is usually present in the blood in low numbers). The first time I read it through, I said out loud (in the pri-vacy of my office), "I have no idea!" I was especially alarmed because I knew this CPC would represent my first real public exposure in Oregon, that I was likely to be scrutinized by house staff and faculty alike as the new honcho from UCLA, and that essentially, I had no choice but to nail it.

The result was that I read hundreds of papers, spent weekends in the library, slept poorly, sweated, ignored other pressing responsibilities (like writing grant proposals), and finally formulated my opinion as to what had ailed this poor young man—an opinion, I might add, that worried me greatly, because the diag-nosis I had chosen had been reported in the medical literature in only twelve patients in the entire world. Could they truly have presented me with a problem so rare and esoteric; and what were the odds that such a case had actually turned up in Oregon?

Before I knew it, September 18 was upon me and the house was packed. As I had feared, anticipation was high. I had decided to approach the case from the point of view of the differential diagnosis of eosinophilia since that was the most dramatic aspect of the case and one that related to my area of expertise. And doing it that way would mean that even if I got the diagnosis wrong, the audience would take home an appreciation of what disorders may underlie an increase in these flashy cells.

I managed a few introductory quips, went on to inform the audience that Eos was the Greek goddess of the dawn, Mother of Memnon, and that her name had been given to the brilliant red cell we call the eosinophil. I went on to describe what we know about the structure, function, and regulation of this remarkable cell (not very much), and then finally got down to cases—working my way through the differential possibilities, excluding each one for hopefully cogent reasons—and as I went, painting myself into an ever smaller corner.

The lecture hall where the CPCs are held has sliding blackboards that one pulls down to write on, and that are obscured when they are in the retracted position. I had listed the common causes of eosinophilia on the first board (mostly infections and allergies), less likely ones on the second (inflammatory disorders, including an inflammatory response to neoplasia), and on a third, a list of neoplastic disorders (carcinomas, plasma cell dyscrasias, lymphomas, and lymphoblastic leukemia). Thus, as I worked my way through the first blackboard, the audience could not see the second and third blackboards—that is, they couldn't see where my analysis was headed and where it would end up. I finally pulled down the last board, explained why possibilities A, B, and C did not fit the case, waffled between D and E, and at the last minute, crossed off D and said, "I therefore believe that the procedure that was performed was a bone marrow aspiration and biopsy, and that it revealed the surprise finding of acute lymphoblastic leukemia."

To my delight, before the pathologist got up to speak—and therefore, before the audience knew if I was right or wrong—there was a spontaneous eruption of loud and lengthy applause. This meant to me that they appreciated the logic of my approach and had learned from my discussion, independent of whether or not it was correct.

Dr. Barbara Hardy, the pathologist, then rose, paused, and said, "John, how much is this worth to you?" "I'll take my medicine," I said. Another pause, and then, "Well, your medicine's mighty good, because you got it exactly right." There was an audible gasp from the audience and an unbelievable sigh of relief from me. Fitchen had arrived at the U of O Medical Center.

I walked on air for the next week, was patted on the back, congratulated, told that my job here was secure forever (way over the top in my opinion, but hey, don't look a gift horse in the mouth). Residents I'd never met came up to me and told me that they'd been going to these things for years and had never heard a CPC that was half as good. One colleague hailed it as "a paradigm." Interns, apparently unable to speak, simply smiled at me.

I'm obviously pleased, proud, and relieved that it went so well, but I don't get paid to be famous in

Gresham (Portland suburb), so I have plowed into writing grant proposals—which, after all, are the life blood of my research effort and my principal value to the institution. I made the October 1 deadline for the Oregon Division of the American Cancer Society, and the October 6 deadline for the VA Merit Review renewal, which leaves only the NIH grant—and I have until November 1 to get that in.

Through all of this frenetic activity, Ellen has been a rock—tolerant of late arrivals, weekends at the hospital, a preoccupied spouse. How she has managed, I can't imagine, because Matthew has been at his most demanding—clearly two. He's learned how to crawl out of his crib and has prompted us to remove one of the sides so that he doesn't have a four-foot fall to the floor after he gets over the side. Of course, he has also mastered the doorknob and the "child-proof" plastic cover for same, which is supposed to keep him from opening the door. He has taken essentially no nap for the past two weeks because he enjoys "escaping" so much, and appears at our bedside at all hours of the night. We figure eventually he'll realize that naptime and nighttime are for sleeping, and that even Houdini had to rest.

Good to get caught up. Hope we can talk on the phone ere long.

Love,
John

One of the most gratifying aspects of my tenure at OHSU was participating each year in the sophomore pathophysiology series. The idea was to teach second-year medical students the basic science underlying clinical medicine, and to do it in a way that helped them see connections between basic science and the bedside. In my case, the particular area of study was blood, cancer, and the reticuloendothelial (immune and inflammatory) system—or, as the course was called at the time, Blood/RES. It was a team effort shared with a distinguished and committed faculty—among them Dick Jones, Bob Koler, Jim Regas, Scott Goodnight, Bob Bigley, and Grover Bagby. We took it seriously, paid attention to student feedback, and were honored, several years in a row, by receiving the award for Pathophysiology Course of the Year.

Jim Regas, the course director, had to be away one year during the last week of our scheduled time slot (one of his daughters was graduating from medical school) and I was volunteered to stand in as acting director in his absence. This meant that all student feedback, including feedback on the final exam, was directed to me. It was clear from the comments of the students that they liked the course a lot—but that they were, shall we say, less than enthusiastic about the final exam. One student, for example, called the exam "a real Jamshidi needle"—a clever reference to the rather medieval-looking implement with which often-painful bone marrow biopsies are performed.

While the students were generally disgruntled with the test's perceived irrelevance to clinical medicine, special invective was reserved for a particular question about blood coagulation. Getting the correct answer to this question required that they know whether activation of vitamin K-dependent clotting factors was accomplished by the binding of GLA residues to the N terminus or the C terminus of the factor molecules. In retrospect, the clinical relevance of this kernel of knowledge *is* a bit obscure.

As acting course director, I was invited to their class banquet to receive the award for course of the year. The class president, who had had a drink or three, gave me a rather cool introduction and reluctantly handed over the award while mumbling thinly veiled references to the final exam. Well aware of the animus about the exam, I stood before the group with an unnerving sense of trepidation.

I said to them, "We are honored, once again, to receive this accolade for course of the year, especially because I know that many of you have questioned the clinical relevance of the final exam. In particular, I've received comments on a question about the activation of clotting factors—about binding of residues to the N terminus or the C terminus. All I can say is that next fall when you go out on the wards and you're standing at the bedside pulling on a rectal glove, you'd better know whether to put your finger in the N terminus or the C terminus."

They laughed. And they let us keep the award.

Teaching was the most fun aspect of academic medicine, but research was the most exciting—for when it works, it creates new knowledge. It could also be profoundly humbling. After Ellen and I returned to Oregon from UCLA, I added a new focus to my investigative effort. Through a mutual friend, Art Vandenbark (an immunologist at the

Portland VA), I met Al Ferro, a biochemist / microbiologist at Oregon State University. He was working with plants and fungi on a compound called methylthioadenosine (MTA) and the enzyme that degrades it, MTA phosphorylase (MTAase). Through this process, the essential amino acid methionine is regenerated.

At first blush, this seemed to have little connection to the bone marrow work being conducted in my lab. But then I learned that Dr. Ferro had been approached by Mike Riscoe, a grad student, about the notion of studying MTA metabolism in mammalian cells. This was of interest to me because it dealt with a fundamental metabolic process—methionine recycling—that might contribute to the regulation of blood cell production under normal conditions, and the lack of regulation underlying leukemic transformation (i.e., when bone marrow cells morph into leukemic cells, leading to this form of blood cancer).

Ferro, Riscoe, and I had some animated discussions about how we might fruitfully combine our areas of expertise: Ferro—biochemistry and enzymology; Fitchen—bone marrow culture, cellular differentiation, access to clinical specimens; Riscoe—hands-on design and execution of experiments. We agreed to collaborate. I would hire Mike as a post-doc as soon as possible to spearhead the project in my lab.

The most exciting project (at least for me) had to do with a novel approach to treating leukemia. The basic idea was to kill leukemic cells by restricting methionine in the diet (which is the only source of this essential amino acid) and rescuing normal cells by administering MTA. The idea was that MTAase-containing normal cells could use supplemental MTA to produce methionine, while

Left to right: the author, Al Ferro, and Mike Riscoe in the lab (photo by © John M. Vincent)

MTAase-deficient leukemic cells could not. This theory seemed to work in test tubes using MTAase-containing and -deficient cell lines. In other experiments, we were able to show that when healthy rats were fed a methionine-free diet, they lost up to 30 percent of their weight in a month, and demonstrated ruffled coats and reduced activity. In contrast, when healthy rats were fed methionine-free diets supplemented with MTA, they gained over 40 percent body weight and maintained smooth coats and normal levels of activity.

Thus the stage was set for the critical experiment: to inoculate rats with a fatal dose of leukemia cells and maintain them on a methionine-free diet supplemented by MTA. To make a long story short, what had worked *in vitro* failed in rats. After much soul searching, we decided that Mike should refocus his effort on applications of methionine recycling to infectious diseases, most notably malaria. As that work has evolved over the years, he has become a major player in the design and development of new anti-malarial drugs through an organization called the Medicines for Malaria Venture, funded in large part by the Gates Foundation. He is now a career research scientist at the VA and a professor of molecular microbiology and immunology at the OHSU School of Medicine. I am very proud of him.

The most fulfilling aspect of academic medicine is patient care. In this role, all the years of learning about human physiology and pathology are brought to bear on the diagnosis and treatment of a single patient. Based on the patient's chief complaint, medical history, physical examination, and preliminary lab tests, the doctor generates a differential diagnosis—a short list of conditions that could account for all the findings and define a pathway to determine a definitive diagnosis for that patient. I would do the same thing when I became a serious birder: carefully noting the "physical findings" of a particular bird in order to make a definitive identification.

Most of my clinical activities were carried out at the VA—in its heyday at the time—which was just a short walk across the sky bridge that connected the University and VA Hospitals. Because of my time as a flight surgeon,

I felt a connection with my patients—many of them, like me, had served during the Vietnam War, and a lot of them, unlike me, had fought in Southeast Asia. I admired and respected them for their courage and their sacrifice. It meant a lot to me to find a way to help them, to fix their ailing bodies, to support them on their journey back to something like normal. They were, and are, brave men and women, worthy of the homage of a grateful nation.

They remain in my thoughts, all of them. One in particular taught me a profound and lasting lesson, which I have shared over and over with medical students on the wards: *always listen to the patient*. This may seem obvious, but it often gets lost in the chaos of admission, the flurry of activity to collect historical information, carry out a physical examination, perform blood draws, start IVs, and obtain EKGs (all of this done, back then, by house staff—interns and residents).

One night, a sixty-year-old World War II veteran was admitted with a chief complaint of "I feel like I have a hole in my head." It was noted in his preliminary lab test results that he was mildly anemic, had a slightly elevated serum protein level, and evidence of a previous silent myocardial infarction (heart attack without chest pain). We homed in on working up his anemia and put in a cardiology consultation for good measure.

Two days later, the situation was no clearer. The house staff were planning to discharge him later that day and follow up on his anemia in clinic. I leafed through the patient's chart and happened to notice his chief complaint, apparently lost in the shuffle. I suggested to the resident and a couple of medical students that we go talk with the patient before we send him home. At the bedside

I asked him if he had any questions for us. He looked up at me and said, "Well, yeah, Doc. I still feel like I have a hole in my head." I palpated his scalp and noted that there was, indeed, a somewhat softer area of his scalp over his left frontal cortex.

We decided to keep the patient in the hospital to work up the "hole in the head." For starters, we sent him to radiology to get an x-ray of the cranium. Sure enough, this revealed a perfectly round, silver dollar-sized, lytic lesion—essentially a punched-out hole—over the left frontal area of the brain. We obtained a neurosurgery consult and a biopsy of the lesion was performed. This revealed a so-called solitary plasmacytoma—a localized tumor of the bone and bone marrow. It was akin to multiple myeloma, but localized. He was subsequently treated and cured with radiation therapy to the affected portion of the skull.

Back in the doctors' office with the resident and students, I looked at them and said, "So?"

Without missing a beat, they chimed in unison, "Always listen to the patient."

In 1985, I was appointed to a search committee to find a new associate chief of staff for research (ACOS/R or just ACOS) at the VA. Dr. John Kendall had left that post to become the dean at the school of medicine. In the course of the search process, I learned in detail about the ACOS position, an administrative job about which I had hardly any previous knowledge. After six months of searching for and interviewing potential candidates, the committee came up with a shortlist of eight, which was then narrowed down to three finalists. It turned out all three were too expensive, with contract conditions and requirements beyond our means. Barry Bell, the hospital director, instructed the committee to start over.

Now aware of the assets and influence that came with this major administrative post, I resigned from the search committee and threw my hat in the ring as a candidate. To my amazement and delight, I was chosen. The position came with extraordinary advantages, most notably 45,000 square feet of sparkling new laboratory space in the new research building—all of it under my control. Upon taking office, I quickly learned that the power to allocate space is extraordinary. When I started, I thought I would spend most of my time talking about money—wrong! Far more important than money is space—a measure of a researcher's value and importance. There's an old joke that two researchers can fill an infinite amount of space—they're always worried the other guy has or will get more.

What proved to be another extraordinary asset was so-called "activation equipment." Denis Burger, PhD, who had served as acting ACOS/R during the search, was a no-paper kind of guy. To streamline the transition process, he cleaned out the filing cabinets in the ACOS office— every last paper folder, save one. This folder contained a copy of a memo from VA Central Office in Washington. The language was a bit dense, but it seemed to be saying that VA administrators realized that newly constructed VA facilities would need to be properly equipped. At the end, it gave a mailing address and information on how to make requests.

I called together five or six of my most trusted colleagues and told them I'd like to put together a modest equipment request and see what happened. We worked on it for a couple of days and ended up with a two-page document that totaled about $400,000 worth of new equipment. We sent it off to DC. Nothing happened until six months later, when out of nowhere, I received a response in the form of a brief three-column memo. The requested items were listed in a column on the left, the associated costs were listed in the column down the middle, and the relevant action was listed on the right. For example,

Hot Plate	$40	*Disapproved*
Tabletop Centrifuge	$8,000	*Approved*
Ultracentrifuge	$30,000	*Approved*
Pipettor	$100	*Disapproved*
Laminar Flow Hood	$10,000	*Approved*

I was stunned. I read the memo. And then I read it again. This looked like an amazing bonanza.

Well, on deeper reflection, the grand bonanza was the new research building—the activation equipment would make that new space hum with the sounds of biomedical research. Together the building and the equipment were an extraordinary catalyst, a motivator, a facilitator. I sent a memo to all the funded investigators in the research service, telling them that it looked like we had identified a mechanism for acquiring new equipment in association with "activation" (the VA, bless their hearts, could never just say "opening") of the new facility. Thank you, Denis Burger, for saving exactly the right memo!

I asked them to let me know what they needed, and to think big. To make a long story short, over the next three years we received $8 million in new equipment—including the machinery necessary to establish a first-class molecular biology lab (DNA sequencer, DNA synthesizer, oligonucleotide synthesizer, and more).

My job as ACOS/R was to create an environment conducive to inquiry and discovery, and to stimulate collaboration and collegiality. I was given exceptional tools to work with, and exceptional people to make the VA research program simmer and bubble and sing. During my five years in the role, our annual competitive research funding rose from $2 million to $10 million (not including activation equipment), the number of funded principal investigators climbed from 20 to 75, and the number of employees grew from 70 to 230. We also established a non-profit foundation under 501(c)(3) status to facilitate flexible management of research funds. Foundation assets grew from nothing to $1.5 million in eighteen months.

Oh—and during this journey, I was promoted to full professor. This was notable to me because I had done it faster than my dad. On hearing the news, he was nonplussed, and grumbled something about soft criteria in academic medicine. It's okay—he was and always will be a better scholar than I. He figured out how they built Cheops's pyramid, for Pete's sake.

FIELD NOTES

A largish sparrow seen at the Sea Scout base on Marine Drive on 11/24/14. Rich rufous crown and eye-ring, bi-colored bill, gray face and neck, rufous epaulets, white wing bars. Central dark chest patch not well seen (but present in photos taken by others); seemed to be very dependent on angle of viewing.

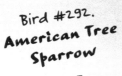

Bird #292.
American Tree Sparrow
[code-5]

CHAPTER 14
A PREDICTION

When the new Portland VA Medical Center and research annex were dedicated in April of 1987, Barry Bell, the hospital director, asked me to write a piece on the future of biomedical research for inclusion in a time capsule. It was to be buried at the dedication and unearthed fifty years later—in 2037. It was typical of Barry to assign projects like this, simultaneously challenging and cool. Thirty-one years into the fifty-year time span, it would appear that I got some things right, and some things sort of right— while other things await developments. I'll leave it to you to make the call. Here's what I wrote:

Biomedical Research in the Year 2037

In contemplating the nature of biomedical research in the year 2037, we might do well first to think *backward*—to what a researcher in the year 1937 might have imagined about the state of medical science in the year 1987. Smug in the recent discovery of penicillin, this hypothetical researcher of 1937 may have envisioned (accurately) a great age of therapeutics, and may even have imagined all human disease would yield to the inexorable progress of biomedical science. Out of humility, the scientists of 1937 may not have viewed themselves as at the pinnacle of biomedical understanding, but nonetheless may have believed they were well up the slopes, close to the summit, obscured only by a few wispy clouds. Back then, the biomedical nature of the genetic code (DNA) was unknown, organ transplantation had not occurred, and computers had not been manufactured. Today, these developments are a reality.

Thus, we are armed in 1987 with the tools of genetic engineering, the nascent ability to manipulate the immune system, and the extraordinary power of computer technology. Though well equipped for the ascent, we are nowhere near the summit of understanding. We have managed, perhaps, to set up a biomedical base camp, and can begin to turn our heads upward, to begin to ponder the great questions of human biology. To predict how far we will progress in the coming fifty years is an exercise in rank speculation—an exercise, nonetheless, which may serve to order our priorities. Therefore, with these provisos in place, let us take the plunge.

By the year 2037, the entire human genome will be sequenced and the function and regulation of many individual genes will be determined. As a result, gene therapy will be commonplace in medical practice. "Gene machines" will produce genetic material tailored to "home" to the proper chromosomal site and correct acquired and inherited genetic abnormalities. Embryogenesis and cellular differentiation will be sufficiently understood to allow the generation *in vitro* of organ systems from a single cell. Manipulation of histocompatibility genes will allow transplantation across previously prohibitive barriers. Blood cells from newborns may be cryopreserved for subsequent production of "replacement parts" for worn-out or diseased organs. Biomechanical engineering will combine microelectronics to produce integrated synthetic nervous systems that will allow paraplegics to walk and quadriplegics to play the piano. Our understanding of learning, memory, behavior, and even emotion will have advanced to a biochemical level, and drugs to alter these phenomena will have been developed.

As disease after disease falls before the march of therapeutic innovation, medical research will turn increasingly to the question of biologic aging. Freed or cured of disease, what are the biological limits of the human system? By the year 2037, this may be the grand question of mammalian biology. What are the genetic controls and biochemical processes which mediate aging? Are these processes subject to alteration? Can they be retarded or even reversed? Is there a biological fountain of youth? Researchers exploring these frontiers may come up against the conundrums of thermodynamic laws: since the law of entropy dictates that disorganization of any closed system must increase over time, indefinite postponement of aging may be biophysically impossible.

From the undoubtedly naïve vantage point of 1987, two things seem clear. First, biomedical science will progress to a deeper biophysical level of understanding over the next fifty years. Researchers of the twenty-first century will probably explore aspects of atomic and sub-atomic medicine. Perhaps the physicians of 2037 will not prescribe medicinals but will send their patients for treatments in electromagnetic fields designed to rectify molecular abnormalities. Second, bioethics will play an increasingly central role in the progress of biological science.

As we have the ability not only to cure disease but also to modulate basic physiological processes such as aging and human behavior, the disciplines of medical science, philosophy, sociology, religion, and political thought will become progressively interrelated and inter-dependent. The ethicists and the public at large may have to decide whether an athlete who received an infusion of genes that promote coordination deserves an Olympic gold medal or whether a scientist who took intelligence-enhancing drugs deserves the Nobel Prize. By the year 2037, there may be the ability to produce "super humans." It is conceivable that society will yield to this temptation in order that mankind not become subservient to computers with artificial intelligence.

The power of computers and biotechnology notwithstanding, human involvement has been essential to scientific progress for centuries and will continue to be so. Intellectual curiosity, creativity, and scientific interchange will remain the most important forces driving biomedical research in the year 2037 and beyond.

FIELD NOTES

A tiny nuthatch discovered at Gabriel Park on 11/3/15 by Jay Withgott. Well-heard: a series of high-pitched pips in doublets and singlets. A very small bird with creamy chest and belly. Sharply demarcated brown head further accentuated by black line through eye. Short tail. Finally got the bird after nineteen trips to Gabriel Park.

Bird #293. **Pygmy Nuthatch**

[Mult First Record; Code-5]

CHAPTER 15
EPITOPE AND HIV

An epitope, also known as an antigenic determinant, is the part of an antigen that is capable of eliciting an immune response and is recognized by the immune system—specifically by antibodies, B cells, and T cells—when the epitope is combined with the specific antibody produced by such a response. That's a mouthful, I know. Suffice it to say, epitopes are central to the immune system in disease states and for use in laboratory procedures.

"Epitope" also became the name given to a biotech start-up based in Beaverton, Oregon, that discovered and developed an oral fluid testing system for HIV. It began as an OHSU laboratory division established in 1974 to perform Human Leukocyte Antigen (HLA) testing for paternity analysis and organ transplantation.

The HLA paternity/organ transplantation service was run by Denis Burger, PhD (director—and, yes, the same guy who served as acting ACOS/R at the VA before I was appointed to that post), Andy Goldstein (manager), and Michael Hubbard (lab tech), plus four or five additional techs. When, in 1979, the university decided to discontinue this service because of liability concerns, Burger, Goldstein, and Hubbard formed a partnership called Immunologic Associates to provide HLA testing. Each put in $500 and the company was born.

The timing was prophetic. Just around the corner, in the summer of 1981, the first cases of acquired immunodeficiency syndrome (AIDS) were noticed by public health officials in California and New York. Over the next several years, as the pace and extent of the AIDS epidemic exploded on the national and global medical scene, companies rushed to develop blood tests to diagnose this horrific and usually fatal disease. The testing procedure that emerged was a two-step algorithm consisting of a screening test for human immunodeficiency virus (HIV) called an ELISA (enzyme-linked immunosorbent assay), followed, if the ELISA was positive, by a substantially more complicated confirmatory test called a western blot. All these tests were based on detection of *antibodies against the virus*, not the virus itself.

Sustained by revenues from organ transplant and paternity testing, Immunologic Associates decided to look into HIV testing. While many companies were working on new and improved ELISA tests, few had the experience or expertise to tackle western blot testing, a more challenging technology with a considerably smaller market. This was just the sort of thing that fit a nimble, small company with the relevant expertise—a company like Immunologic Associates.

After careful deliberation, the decision was made to send Andy Goldstein to an intensive one-week course on HIV western blot testing sponsored by the Center for Disease Control in Atlanta. Through this channel, he not only gained valuable technical experience, but also made critical connections for access to viral lysates (a source of HIV proteins) as well as to blood samples from affected patients. Bottom line: Immunologic Associates had all the tools necessary to develop a high-performance HIV western blot—a growing and critical need for protecting the blood supply.

The missing piece was funding. The original $1,500 was obviously long gone, and revenues from HLA typing were dwindling as paternity testing was increasingly based on DNA testing. They needed some real money. So they decided to go public. On November 12, 1986, Immunologic Associates changed its name to Epitope, Inc., and made an initial public offering on the American Stock Exchange under the call sign EPT that raised $3 million.

Developing the HIV serum western blot was the centerpiece of the company's business plan, a promising strategy largely because the FDA regulatory pathway was manageable and the need was great. The test would be used only to monitor and protect the blood supply, not to make a diagnosis of HIV infection. As a result, it would be reviewed by the FDA Center for Biologics Evaluation and Research as a Class II medical device—a moderate process compared to the arduous review applied to a diagnostic test (Class III).

Ultimately, the FDA gave approval to several regional labs (including Epitope) to perform HIV confirmatory testing in conjunction with blood bank operations. This propelled a second round of funding (this one for $6 million) which was carried out on May 2, 1989. The following year, Al Ferro (my colleague from Oregon State University) was recruited to join Epitope as its vice president for research. Shortly thereafter, I received an urgent call from Ferro asking if we could meet immediately.

He told me that the company was under duress. The board had called an emergency meeting to review allegations that Denis Burger had been comingling time and funds between Epitope and Yamhill Valley Vineyards, an enterprise founded and owned by Burger. The outcome was that Burger and Hubbard were fired and Ferro was installed as the new CEO. He asked if I would consider becoming the medical director and vice president for research and clinical activities. He said he needed help right away, the help of someone he could trust.

Now in my fifth year at the VA, I had played an active role in putting Portland VA research on the map. Portland VA research was fiscally sound and intellectually thriving. It felt like a reasonable time to step aside and let someone else drive the boat. Among other things, I welcomed the opportunity to work on the development and marketing of products that could be of immediate benefit—that could save lives now, or at least soon. It was also reassuring that Epitope had recently carried out a large round of funding and therefore had staying power.

So I said yes to Al's offer. I was then, and remain today, full of good feelings about my time as the ACOS/R at the Portland VA Medical Center. In that post, I got to work with bright, committed men and women who engaged in top-notch biomedical science, and who experienced the joy of creating new knowledge.

As soon as I had accepted the position at Epitope, Al Ferro, Andy Goldstein, and I sat down for a thorough review of the projects on the books at the company. There were more than twenty. We were stunned. A company our size could not possibly afford such an expansive and ill-focused research and development portfolio—we *had* to focus. From the twenty-plus possibilities, we selected five, reviewed them in great detail a second time, then picked the one with the most promising outlook—based on feasibility, progress to date, and market potential.

Turns out Andy had been doing some work on the side (not even on the list of twenty), exploring a new approach to sample collection and testing for HIV that would use oral fluid rather than blood for diagnosis. The key was *oral fluid*—or more precisely, oral mucosal transudate—*not* saliva. In his puttering, Andy had discovered that he could collect fluid from the gingival crevices of the oral cavity (where the gum meets the tooth) that were enriched for IgG antibodies—the type that reacts with HIV proteins. In other words, this fluid from the mucosal tissue of an infected individual contains antibodies produced by the immune system to fight that infection—in this case the human immunodeficiency virus.

With further refinements of the collection procedure and the addition of preservatives and reagents to prevent sample degradation and non-specific binding, he was able to obtain samples with a hundredfold increase in IgG antibodies. He even had a name for it—OraSure. The hundredfold increase was well within the range of

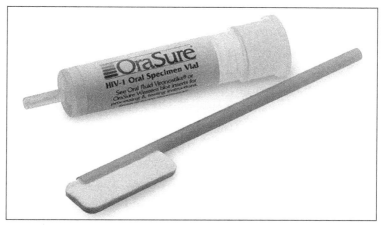

The OraSure specimen collection device: treated pad, stick, and preservative-containing vial

antibody concentration needed for ELISA screening and even western blot confirmatory testing. With the HIV epidemic raging on, OraSure's ability to provide non-invasive sample collection had great promise—first and foremost as a powerful tool in the war against HIV, but also as a medical product with considerable market potential.

The OraSure algorithm involved three components: the device to collect and preserve the oral fluid sample; the ELISA screen to test the fluid for HIV antibodies; and, if that was positive, the western blot confirmatory test.

This ingenious solution (an alternative to blood collection and testing) was classic Andy Goldstein. We used to kid him about his approach to problems. Most of us mere mortals, when going from point A to point B, look straight ahead and focus on point B, trying not to deviate from the most direct route. Andy, on the other hand, would take a step or two down the path to B, and then look off to the left and say, "Hey, what's that?" And after he'd checked out the situation to the left, he'd return to the main path, take a few more steps, look off to the right and say, "Hey, what's this?" and take a few steps in that direction. It was by just such a thought process that he stumbled further down one of his sidetracks, and the result was OraSure. This, my friends, is the stuff of genius, of unrelenting curiosity. It is the road to discovery.

Shortly after deciding to focus on oral fluid testing for HIV, we appointed Daniel Malamud, PhD, a professor of medicine and dental medicine at the University of Pennsylvania, to serve on the Epitope Scientific Advisory Board. His background and research were a perfect fit. The word was he knew everything there was to know about the oral cavity, and in particular, he was engaged in the development of microfluidic point-of-care tests for HIV, utilizing oral fluid. In October 1992, he organized, together with the New York Academy of Sciences, a symposium on this topic. With conceptual assistance from Dan, we put together (and handed

Matt (*left*) and Marty Fitchen showing off their new T-shirts

out at the meeting) promotional T-shirts. I brought two home for my boys, who displayed them with great energy and élan—a symbol, they told me, of the spirit of Epitope.

Before proceeding with the story of OraSure, it is worthwhile to present a brief overview of the HIV/AIDS epidemic then and now, to review the global impact of this devastating disease, to understand the importance of identifying and later treating it. To that end, what follows is assembled from reports by the CDC, WHO, and UNAIDS.

During the summer of 1981, healthcare professionals in California and New York noticed that previously healthy gay men were getting sick with opportunistic infections, including a rare lung infection, *Pneumocystis carinii* pneumonia, and a rare cancer, Kaposi's sarcoma. By year-end, 270 cases of severe immune deficiency had been reported in gay men, 121 of whom had died. Nearly a year later, the term AIDS (acquired immunodeficiency syndrome) was used for the first time, and the disease had been identified in people who injected drugs, transfusion patients, infants, and women with sexual partners who had AIDS. And yet no cause was identified until mid-1984, when French and American researchers announced that they had found the virus that causes AIDS—HTLV-III, renamed HIV in mid-1986.

A blood test was approved to screen for the virus in 1985, and by the end of that year, every region in the world had reported at least one case of AIDS, with 20,303 cases in total. The only measure available to combat the spread of the disease was prevention—abstinence, condom use, needle exchanges—and testing was a crucial element in the fight: to identify those who were infected and harness the opportunity to educate them.

Finally, in 1990, the FDA approved the first drug to treat AIDS—AZT—for use in children. But the numbers continued to explode: by the end of that year, more than 307,000 AIDS cases had been officially reported, with the actual number estimated to be closer to a million. Eight to ten million people were thought to be living with HIV worldwide.

In June 1995, the FDA approved the first protease inhibitor, beginning a new era of highly active antiretroviral treatment. At last, a major turning point in the treatment of HIV/AIDS. At the National Candlelight AIDS March in Washington, DC, in 1996, I heard from people with AIDS who had given up, sold their homes, given away their pets, said goodbye to friends and family. But with access to protease inhibitors, their lives had suddenly improved—they had futures, and lives to look forward to living. New drug development continued, offering new hope, and, importantly, testing was a vital step in getting drugs to people who needed them. OraSure could play a key role in that process.

Back to 1991. The first major hurdle in the process of developing and commercializing OraSure was to determine the regulatory pathway required by the FDA. Unlike the serum western blot that would be used only for protecting the blood supply, OraSure samples would be used specifically for diagnosis. This had major regulatory consequences.

We met with officials at the agency and were told that because OraSure would be used for diagnostic purposes, it would be reviewed as a Class III medical device under rules and regulations of the Center for Devices and Radiologic Health. But the review itself would be carried out by the Center for Biologics Evaluation and Research (CBER). This rather arcane arrangement was prompted by the fact that CBER regulated products dealing with the blood supply (through its Division of Emerging and Transfusion Transmitted Diseases, directed by Jay Epstein, MD), and much of their in-house expertise was relevant to HIV and AIDS.

Over the next three-and-a-half years, we would work closely with Dr. Epstein and his staff, trying to find a regulatory pathway that would address the concerns of the varied constituents who had a stake in the growing epidemic. We knew, and the FDA knew, that there was a lot of hysteria surrounding the disease. But there was also the alarming and frightening reality: the continued spread of HIV/AIDS in the gay community, healthcare workers, hemophiliacs, sex workers, and the population at large.

As the epidemic progressed, it was clear that OraSure would have a positive impact. It was non-invasive (no needles, no risk to health workers), simple (requiring little or no training), and portable (sample collection could be accomplished in the field). Indeed, with OraSure there was the chance for the so-called "teachable moment."

Say, for example, that a social worker was meeting with an injection drug user or commercial sex worker and discussing the need for frequent HIV testing. In the past, that would have required scheduling a clinic visit for a blood draw, showing up for the blood draw, then returning to the clinic a week later to receive and discuss the results. With OraSure, none of that was necessary. On the spot, the social worker would say, "Here, just place this pad between your cheek and gum for two minutes. I'll take the sample to the lab for testing and meet you back here tomorrow to discuss the results."

We argued during interactions with the FDA that requiring extensive clinical trials would substantially decelerate entry of a powerful tool in the fight against HIV/AIDS. In negotiations with FDA staff, we asserted that the potential benefits of OraSure far outweighed any risks, and that clinical trials should be modest in scope and numbers. We lost.

The study that ultimately emerged involved 3,570 subjects: 2,382 at low risk, 698 at high risk, 242 with diagnosed AIDS, and 248 "non-specificity" subjects—persons with diseases associated with an increased frequency of false-positive results. Samples were collected at eleven geographically diverse sites, including blood banks, public health clinics, general medical clinics, HIV clinics, sexually transmitted disease clinics, and a hemophilia center, all in the United States.

The results were remarkable. They indicated that HIV testing of OraSure samples was highly accurate. In the entire study population of 3,570 subjects, the results obtained from following the testing algorithm were correct for all but one individual, a late-stage AIDS patient whose ELISA was non-reactive. The likely explanation for this single false-negative is that in late-stage infection, the patient's immune system crashes and is no longer able to produce anti-HIV antibodies—so there's nothing for the ELISA to detect. Thus, in more than 99.9% of subjects, either the correct result was obtained with the initial OraSure sample, or appropriate follow-up testing would be triggered.

As the astounding clinical trials results sank in, and as the vibes from FDA were increasingly favorable, it became clear that we needed to scale up production for product launch immediately following approval. Al called me to his office and told me he was putting me in charge of ramping up OraSure manufacturing—currently standing at a mere one hundred devices per day (to be used for quality control and stability testing) and produced manually in the boardroom by two grandmas working part-time. Al said the initial goal was to increase production in six weeks to 50,000 devices per week while initiating required good manufacturing practices (GMPs), and cutting costs. He gave me carte blanche—any resources I needed he would provide—all I had to do was ask.

I assigned Becky Keizur, a capable and committed employee from the Product Development Department as the project manager for this endeavor. We contracted with two engineers who were given whatever resources they needed to produce mechanized machinery to assemble the device—that is, to attach the treated cotton fiber pad to the plastic stick. We also identified some floor space in an old warehouse nearby. It was old, but it was clean, good enough to meet our needs. We also put together two shifts of workers to carry out the treatment and drying of the pad before assembly. Importantly, all of these people were Epitope employees. There was a growing sense of pulling together—of commitment to a collective and worthwhile mission. That same esprit would propel us in the months and years to come.

One afternoon, Epitope was visited by two financial analysts from New York. We kept steering them to the laboratory, the product development area, and the clinical trials operation. They kept saying they wanted to see the manufacturing area. Since the production line was in an old warehouse building with few amenities, we feared that it would come across as bush-league, and continued to resist. But finally they were so persistent that we had to say yes.

We walked to the warehouse and opened the overhead door. To the great surprise of the employees, two dark suits walked into the building and stopped to soak up the sounds, the lights, and the energy of the manufacturing procedure. They kept coming back to the pad-to-stick assembly machines. "If I've got this right," one of them said, "every time this machine goes *p-chee, p-chew,* it's another $5 in your bank account. If my sense of time and my math are correct, that's $5 every second, $300 every minute, $18,000 every hour, and $288,000 every double shift. Interesting."

As soon as the suits had left, and after a short drive to the bank to pick up some cash, I returned to the warehouse and burst in the door, startling everyone in the room.

"Shut it down," I said, "shut it down. Take the phones off the hooks. I want to tell you something. Our stock went up two full points today (from 10 to 12) and that's because of you, every one of you. It's because of what the suits saw you all doing, making our product, doing it well, with commitment, together. They were very impressed, and so am I. I'm proud of you, proud of what you have accomplished under great pressure. Bravo!" I clapped, they clapped. We clapped together.

I took Becky into the office and closed the door. I handed her an envelope and told her, "This envelope contains $1,000 in cash. It is your discretionary fund, to be used as you see fit. I don't want to hear that the production line is down for lack of an extension cord or a can of WD-40. And if one of the line workers does something special, acknowledge it, celebrate it, and let them know you noticed. Keep it up, Becky. You're doing a great job."

In the months ahead, the company became progressively focused on a document called a PMA, or premarket approval application. When completed, this document would contain a full and detailed description of the OraSure clinical trials, manufacturing procedures, quality control, quality assurance, package insert, facilities, scientific advisors, specialty consultants, and on and on.

It seemed as if we would never be done with the paperwork. The process was arduous and unrelenting. The catch phrase around the company was "PMA 'til ya puke." It got so that those of us who were closest to the clinical trials and data analysis never had to look up sample numbers. When a colleague said a number, we could recite the results. Everybody worked weekends—no one more than Deborah Sherris, who was there six weekends in a row. If you had a question about the data, she would know the answer. Her effort was symbolic of the sustained heavy lifting up and down the corporate ranks.

Finally, in the spring of 1994 it came down to the wire—a self-imposed wire. Essentially, the review process wouldn't begin until we submitted the PMA, so we decided we'd submit, no matter what, by June 18, 1994. Once we submitted, FDA would have 180 days to review and approve, defer, or decline. On the final day, and into the evening hours, a group of us gathered in the "library"—essentially an open space on the second floor—and put the magnum opus together on our hands and knees. It was, in its final form, 1,972 pages long, and we were required to submit ten copies—nearly 20,000 pages of documents in total. Ten people on the floor would add each page or section in order to their pile. Others would distribute the next page, and it would be placed in the pile, and so forth. And when the assembly process was completed, we went back to page one and flipped through the documents to confirm that the pages were complete and in the right order.

During this extended process, it became clear that we weren't going to make the FedEx deadline at the airport (6:00 p.m.). But, hey, this was Epitope, and some enterprising soul had discovered a company called Sonic Air that would accept packages as late as 11:30 p.m. At 11:00, Andy and helpers loaded the trunk of his car and headed for the airport, on the exact opposite end of the city. It was usually a forty-minute drive; he made it in nineteen. Clearly, when he needed to, Andy could go directly from point A to point B, and in this case he made it with time to spare. We all stayed at Epitope, waiting for him to return so that we could celebrate meeting the deadline.

The clock with the FDA was now ticking.

In roughly the same timeframe, we were in discussions with SmithKline Beecham (now GlaxoSmithKline) about a marketing partnership. This was a big deal for us—a very small company (ninety employees) joining forces with a very large one (tens of thousands of employees). Near the end of December, we flew to Pittsburgh to meet with the marketing team at SKB, headed by project manager Donna Sturgess, to discuss the possibilities. These were stirring times. The events surrounding those meetings and the essentially simultaneous approval of OraSure are set forth in a newsletter I composed to be delivered to all the people of Epitope. I felt moved by the company-wide effort, and wanted to share with everyone the behind-the-scenes story of OraSure approval day.

The following events unfolded while we were in Pittsburgh. I recounted these events in the *Epigram*, our Epitope company newsletter, as follows.

[Note: Many of the people and organizations mentioned in this newsletter are identified by first name only or came from outside the company, so I have included a "cast of characters" below to help you navigate. Some of it may be hard to follow, but my hope is to give you a sense of the drama and excitement.]

EPIGRAM

How It All Came Down
By John Fitchen, December 25, 1994

It's Christmas night. All the presents have long since been opened, we've been to the traditional neighborhood party, the kids are upstairs trying out new video games, Ellen's asleep on the sofa. It's quiet—peaceful even. And there is finally a moment to reflect on what's happened in the last four days—to relive the events and the emotions surrounding the approval of OraSure, and to share it with all of you who made it happen.

It began early Wednesday morning at five forty-five, when Al and Kevin and I met at Portland International Airport for our flight to Pittsburgh. Over coffee we speculated about the meaning of the quickened pace with the FDA, and about the rumors that they wanted to get it done by Christmas.

"I'll believe it when I see the approval letter," I said.

"I know," said Al, "but this time it's different. Not only is there a sense of all-out effort at Epitope— there's a sense of all-out effort at the agency, too, not to mention the faxes and phone calls between the FDA and Organon. This may actually happen, and, if it does, we've got to get ready."

We talked on the plane about our plans: about setting up the special phone line for the media, the various possible venues for a short-notice press conference, the outside experts list, the code words for communicating with Andy if we got the word.

CAST OF CHARACTERS *(in alphabetical order)*

Al: Al Ferro (CEO, Epitope)

Andy: Andy Goldstein (VP product development, Epitope)

CBER: (FDA Center for Biologics Evaluation and Research)

Deb: Deb Auter (assistant to Nancy Buc)

Elaine: Elaine DuBesa (VP regulatory affairs, Epitope)

Ellen: Ellen Fitchen (my wife)

FDA: (Food and Drug Administration)

Gil: Gil Miller (CFO, Epitope)

Jan Misley: (travel coordinator, Epitope)

Jay: Jay Ferro (Al's son)

John Fitchen: (VP research/clinical activities, Epitope)

Julie: Julie Ferro (Al's wife)

Katharine: Katharine Lawrence (my right hand, Epitope)

Kathy Zoon and Jay Epstein: (FDA higher-ups)

Kevin: Kevin Crowley (VP marketing, Epitope)

Marty: Marty Fitchen (my younger son)

Mary: Mary Hagen (executive assistant to CEO, Epitope)

Mary Pendergast and Amanda Pedersen: (FDA commissioner's office)

Matthew: Matthew Fitchen (my elder son)

Mike Francis: (reporter for the *Oregonian*)

Nancy: Nancy Buc (DC-based regulatory counsel)

Organon: Organon Teknika, Inc. (manufacturer of OraSure ELISA)

Peggy Miller: (Gil Miller's wife)

Roger Pringle: (chairman of the board, Epitope)

Sharon Geyer: (FDA reviewer assigned to our application)

Steve Weiner: (PR media consultant for Epitope)

Tom Clement: (regulatory affairs director at Organon)

When we arrived in Pennsylvania, I called Elaine. She was camped out in DC and had been in almost hourly contact with Sharon Geyer and others at the FDA. She rattled off a long list of minor changes in labeling and standard operating procedures that the agency wanted finalized overnight.

"Do they need final, mastered documents or just change requests?" I asked.

"They want the final, official paper," Elaine said. "Signed, sealed and delivered."

"Can we do it?"

"Well, everybody is willing to stay up all night if that's what it takes. We'll give it a shot."

Next, I called Tom Clement, the regulatory affairs director at Organon, to see if he had received the marked-up version of their package insert from Sharon Geyer. He told me he finally had (he had originally expected it the day before), and there were problems. "She wants to require that calibration readings are specified in the package insert and recorded by every laboratory each time they test OraSure samples," he told me. But there was good news on another front: the FDA had apparently accepted our arguments and had softened its position on "sample adequacy," a potential sticking point elsewhere in the package insert.

Al, Kevin, Gil (who had hooked up with us on his way back from Europe), and I headed off to dinner with our hosts, knowing that they would ask about the timing of approval, and wondering what we should say. We didn't say much.

The next day (Thursday), we were holed up in a conference room talking future business with our hosts when the phone rang. It was Deb Auter, associate of Nancy Buc, our regulatory counsel in DC.

"FDA wants a conference call with you guys and Nancy at three thirty to discuss conditions of approval," Deb told us. "Nancy's on the Jersey Turnpike on her way back from New York, but we can patch her in on her cell phone."

We asked the people around the conference table if we could have a few minutes to huddle. A three-thirty conference call was going to be touch-and-go because we had a five o'clock plane to catch. Gil called Jan Misley. If we needed more time, we could get an eight o'clock flight to Seattle.

Deb Auter called back and said the FDA wanted more time—could the conference call be at four thirty or five? Gil alerted Jan to switch us to the later flight, and we headed off to the airport where our hosts had lined up a conference room with a speakerphone. The setup was fairly primitive: there was an adequate speakerphone, but the pay fax machine was outside the conference room and the instructions were hard to understand (at least for a bunch of excited executives).

Finally the FDA cover sheet came through on the fax machine. But that was it—cover sheet and nothing else. We thought the machine had run out of paper. Thirty minutes later we finally found someone who could help us. It turned out the rest of the pages were rolled up inside the machine.

Knowing that the conference call was about to begin, we powered through the conditions listed in the fax. No surprises. A few questions of information, but no key issues. Having waited until the last possible minute, Kevin said he had to leave to catch his plane to his mom's. As he zipped out the door, he deadpanned, "This looks pretty good."

We got through to Nancy Buc on the Jersey Turnpike. "Is there anything here we can't live with?" we asked her.

"No, this is great!" she told us. "This should be it."

Five minutes later, the phone rang. "ATT operator with a conference call for Mr. Ferro. Let me take the roll call, please." The operator ticked off the people on the call—Al Ferro; Nancy Buc; Kathy Zoon, Jay Epstein, and others from CBER; and Mary Pendergast and Amanda Pedersen, from the FDA commissioner's office.

We asked a few questions about the conditions. It was clear there was nothing serious in our way. Nancy Buc chimed in. "Not to be presumptuous, but does this mean we can expect a letter in the near future?" FDA was evasive.

"You understand, don't you, that Al is on the East Coast, and that Epitope is closed tomorrow." Tomorrow was Friday, and they hadn't understood that. Maybe it would be a good idea if Al got back to Oregon tonight, they said, because there might be something in the morning.

"How early in the morning? We have to make a coordinated announcement in keeping with SEC rules and guidelines."

FDA said they didn't know about stock-related issues, but finally told us they might issue a letter and a simultaneous public statement as early as seven in the morning (which would be four in the morning for us). Al gave the FDA his home phone number and requested a call if anything was going out before six, Pacific Standard Time. Everybody expressed positive sentiments of mutual effort as the conference call came to a close.

Al, Gil, and I took a deep breath. We had about an hour before we had to catch our plane. Gil checked our tickets and suddenly realized that we (and our luggage) were only booked through to Seattle. He went to call Jan.

Al and I called Steve Weiner, our PR/media consultant in Chicago. "Can you make it to Portland tonight?" we asked him.

"Yeah, there's a nine thirty out of O'Hare," he said. "I should be able to catch that."

We agreed that we would all meet at Epitope at six in the morning. Steve asked if we had notified anyone at the company yet. "We called you first because we knew you had to make travel arrangements, but we're about to call Andy and tell Mary so that the necessary actions can get in motion back there," we told him.

When we reached Andy, the Epitope holiday party was in full swing. "Are you sitting down? Are you alone?" we asked Andy. "Better close your door. We have good news. *The eagle has landed!*"

Andy immediately recognized the code words. "This is fantastic," he said. "Wow!"

"Gotta talk quietly," we said. "This is very sensitive information." Andy told us the party was still going and nobody could hear. We all fantasized about how neat it would be to patch into the PA system and announce the news at the party. Alas, per SEC rules about selective disclosure, that couldn't be. Andy went to get Mary so that media arrangements could be set in motion.

Al and I looked straight at each other. Eye to eye we realized that this was the moment. Approval! We talked about how we shouldn't tell anyone—not even our families—until the news was public. That lasted about two minutes. Al got through to home. Julie was out, Jay was there. With tears streaming down his cheeks, he told his son the happy news. "This is it, Jay, we're off and running now."

Five minutes later, I reached Ellen and told her about the "eagle." She couldn't believe her ears. We agreed that she would wait until bedtime to tell the boys, for fear that they might inadvertently say something to a friend.

Our calls weren't done, but we had to get to the plane. Al, Gil, and I were in the same row, and the minute we got seated, we all started writing. Lists of who to call, and refinements of a press release, letter to stockholders, comments to the media, and plans for how to orchestrate Friday passed from seat to seat as we sipped airline champagne. Gil pecked furiously at his portable computer.

When we reached our cruising altitude, Al called Roger Pringle on the air phone so that Roger could pass the word to the board of directors. As soon as he was off the phone with Roger, Al asked me to call Kevin. I glanced at the businessman sitting next to me. His eyes were half closed, but I was sure he would hear me talking on the phone. "You better make the call," I said to Al, who was sitting on the other side of Gil next to the window. Al got Kevin at his mother's and told him that things looked pretty good. "I want you to activate plans for product roll-out immediately."

We touched down in Seattle on time, relieved that we would make our connection to Portland. Our luggage was another story. Our bags, we were told, had been originally checked through to Seattle, then (hopefully) flagged to go to Portland. We decided to go to the baggage claim in Seattle to see if they turned up there. Gil went to the gate to check us in while Al and I waited. Al's bag and one of Gil's bags popped up. Al headed off with what we had received. I waited. At five minutes before departure, I ran the half-mile to the gate only to find that our flight was delayed—I would make it to Portland, but the arrival of the rest of our luggage would have to rest on providence.

We were met at the Portland Airport by Julie and Jay Ferro and Peggy Miller. Miracle of miracles, and in keeping with the feeling that the gods were on our side, the missing luggage rolled out at the baggage claim.

I pulled up the driveway at around one in the morning, and Marty (my twelve-year-old, who I expected to be long since fast asleep) called out his window, "Way to go, Dad!" And Matthew charged out the door and embraced me in a big bear hug.

I stayed up until two thirty, talking with my family about what had transpired. The alarm clock went off at four thirty, and for once it was easy for me to bounce right out of bed. It was coming down today.

We congregated at six. Al had received a call at five thirty from Kathy Zoon and Jay Epstein saying the letter was signed and was being faxed. It hadn't yet arrived—what was going on? We notified AMEX that we were anticipating a major announcement and wondered if trading in our stock should be halted. AMEX demurred, but then decided to halt trading on their own, because of an uptick in activity.

We called the FDA to ask what was happening. The word was that the letter was coming but had to be "date-stamped and logged out," and that this process might take another hour or two. Finally, somewhere around seven thirty in the morning, the approval letter came. We sat down and read it fast but carefully. Nothing new, no surprises. The press release was a go.

We put out the news. AMEX endeavored to reopen trading, somewhere in the twenty-four to twenty-eight dollar range. I asked Katharine to spread the word, and a most remarkable phenomenon began to happen—people just showed up. As the media blitz swirled, the people of Epitope appeared, and smiled, and cheered, and gave us hugs. We were buoyed by what was happening. A spontaneous celebration, a joyous expression of victory was going on around us. Everybody was hugging—hugging us, hugging each other. We headed off to the press conference, feeling the emotional support of the whole company.

The rest, as they say, is history. The front-page article by Mike Francis in the Saturday *Oregonian*, and then, amazingly, more front-page coverage on Sunday, was incredible and gratifying. I feel tonight like a great thing has happened. I feel like David has overcome Goliath. I'm proud of all of us, and I'm excited by what lies ahead.

– Christmas 1994

A year later, in December 1995, we were waiting to receive notification from the FDA on our oral fluid western blot confirmatory test, the PMA for which had been filed back in June. We had been hoping for a letter from the FDA since December 11, the 180-day PMA review deadline, and had been assured by Ron Maynor (the chair of the FDA review committee) that its arrival was imminent. After a week of being patient, we couldn't wait any longer. (It's always a close call on whether to badger FDA about something you really want to know—you want to know, but you run the risk of annoying the very person who controls the fate of the product.) We huddled and decided that the best action was for Richard George, VP of research, to call Ron Maynor on an informal basis to ask whether the FDA was affected by the budget battle. "Are you guys open for business?" he would say, and then add: "By the way, anything new on our letter?"

Richard came down to my office to report on the call. "It's good news," he said. "Ron told me the letter is finalized, and it's going through the signature process. He said we should have it today or tomorrow morning at the latest."

"Did he give you any idea of what the letter says?" I asked.

"He told me that we wouldn't be unhappy with what the letter says, but he didn't give any specifics."

As I processed the double negative that seemed to add up to a positive, we went to talk to Al. Since we had not yet been inspected, the very best we could hope for was an "approvable" letter. This is a procedure more common than outright approval, by which the FDA lets companies know that a new product, and the clinical trials supporting it, are acceptable. In other words, the product will be approved pending completion of additional tasks. Sometimes the additional tasks are minor. Often they are more involved. But usually they are not *major*, since that would likely beget a so-called "deficiency" letter. We cautiously allowed ourselves to think that Ron Maynor's double negative sounded more like an "approvable" letter than a "deficiency" letter.

Wednesday morning, Richard called Ron Maynor again. He was out. Later, Richard got a voicemail message that the letter was being "firmed up" and that we should have it in the next day or two. Now the gastrointestinal churning began in earnest. "Firmed up"—what the hell did that mean? Was the whole thing back to square one? Were they drafting the letter from scratch? Would delivery of the letter be postponed until after the holidays? We realized, of course, that no matter how much we worried, it would not affect the outcome.

We worried anyway.

By Friday, when Ron Maynor had called to say the letter should be coming "any minute," Al and Richard and I began to move in a fretful pack, checking each of the three fax machines every five to ten minutes. We wondered if our movements would give people a clue that something important was up. Duh! As Nancy Lime, our quality assurance manager, said to me later, "You guys shouldn't walk around in groups. It makes us nervous." Al finally asked me if I wanted to take a long walk outside, reasoning on the "watched pot theory" that unless we left the premises the letter wouldn't come.

We walked for ten minutes. The wind was cold. Screw it, let's go back. We came in the front door and asked the question with our eyes. Sitting behind the reception desk, Paige Khan shook her head—nothing. We trudged upstairs. Mary commented that Al was acting like an expectant father. Al told her it looked like the "birth" would come after the first of the year.

Half an hour later, Paige called my office. "I think I've got what you need," she said calmly. I reached the front desk in seconds. I ran upstairs to make copies, trying to read as I went. It took only two sentences to get the gist:

"The Center for Biologics Evaluation and Research has completed its review of your premarket approval application for OraSure HIV-1 Western Blot Kit. Based upon the information provided in support of your request, your PMA has been found approvable subject to your submission of the following." I tried to read "the following" as the pages flipped through the copier. *Doesn't look like much*, I thought—but I knew the letter had to be read carefully.

I found Al in Andy's office. I closed the door and handed them copies, pointing as I did to the fax cover sheet, upon which was handwritten: "Approvable Letter: BP9S0004." We started reading, and then Al said, "We've got to get out of here. We've got to be able to read this letter thoroughly and thoughtfully without interruption. We've got to know what it says and how we will respond before we start talking about it."

We filed out of Andy's office, trying to conceal our excitement. Again, per SEC rules, until the news was given out in an official press release, we had to keep it secret. Mary was talking to Jan Misley and turned to look right at me. I couldn't help it—I grinned from ear to ear.

We drove to the Marriott Courtyard and pulled up chairs around a table in the lobby. Each of us read through the stipulations line by line. Almost in unison, we said, "This is nothing. What they're asking us to submit is just paperwork." We put names by each of the points. Most of them were for Micki Rahm, our quality assurance director. We made a mental note that we needed her assessment of the

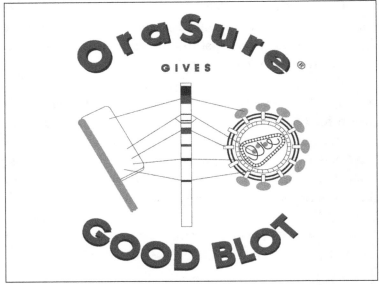

T-shirt design to commemorate approval of OraSure Western Blot—we gave some to the relevant FDA staff, knowing they couldn't wear them in public, but wanting to acknowledge their diligent work on our product

stipulations before we could confidently consider them minor. We read on—approval, as we already knew, was also dependent on passing inspection and negotiation of final labeling. No surprises there. The rest was boilerplate.

As he had almost a year to the day earlier, Al looked me straight in the eye. "Here we go, Dr. Fitchen," he said. "Here we go." We all knew this was big. It meant that we were close to having a complete and compelling product. A non-invasive way to carry out screening *and* confirmatory testing for HIV antibodies. A full algorithm.

We joked about developing a Yuletide tradition with the FDA—two years in a row receiving a key letter on the Friday before Christmas. We said a quiet prayer of thanks to Ron Maynor for his reasonableness and his wisdom in moving our product forward, working it through the review process. We headed back to the office.

When we got there, we tried to enter calmly—business as usual. Mary took one look at us and said, "It's lucky you guys don't work for the CIA." We huddled with Gil, who began working on a press release. I called Donna Sturgess and Ted Kyle at SKB.

A while later, Andy and I got talking about stability testing of the western blot. He told me that in less than two weeks, Product Development would complete twenty-five months of stability testing on the product.

"You mean we've actually got real-time stability data for over two years?" I asked. "What a company!"

Al reappeared with Micki in tow. "I've heard what I need to know," he said. He turned to Micki and nodded for her to give her assessment.

"Hey, piece of cake," she said. "We can get this out in a day!"

It had all been moving pretty fast. In a two-hour period we received the letter, reviewed and nailed down all the particulars, tried repeatedly to contact our partners, and drafted a release announcing the news. There was finally a quiet moment. In that quiet moment, Andy told us about his Chinese dinner Wednesday night and the message inside his fortune cookie. We'd all been so worried by the delay that he hadn't shared it until now. Amazingly, prophetically, it read:

> A letter soon will make you glad,
> 'Twill be the nicest one you've had.

FIELD NOTES

A gull-like bird seen for ten to fifteen seconds flying above the Columbia River on 12/23/15, from 122nd to I-205 bridge, and then over to Government Island, where it disappeared. A very striking bird, even at long range. Direct, level flight (no gliding or soaring), with quick, stiff wingbeats. Bold black "M" pattern across the back, with bright white at mid-wing. Smaller than most gulls. Flew thirty to forty feet above the water in a straight line. Head not well seen, but light overall. wings medium length and somewhat rounded. This ID is on the threshold of tickable, but based on flight pattern, bold "M" on back and light head, it seems reasonable to take the tick.

Bird #294. **Black-Legged Kittiwake**

[Code-5]

CHAPTER 16
PUDKNOCKERS

At first glance, this chapter has little to do with the themes of this book. But in fact, without the events described below, the book would not exist. The very notion of it was derived from discussions during poker evenings with son Marty and his friends—they were the ones who encouraged me to write down my stories. They planted the seed.

When my younger son Marty entered middle school in 1993 he asked me if I would teach him how to play poker. Having played the game a fair amount in college, and with some success, I was open to the idea, but told him I would do so only if we played *real* poker, not the then-emerging high-bluff form of the game called Texas hold 'em. I told him I would teach him the etiquette of the game and what I considered to be classic, non-professional poker: variations on five-card and seven-card poker with names like Anaconda, Mississippi, Chicago, Black Mariah, Push Tittle, Iron Cross, and Five-Card-Lowball-Roll-Your-Own-All-the-Way-with-a-Buy-at-the-End. As an indicator of our intention to play a serious brand of the game, only one of these involves wild cards.

After I had spent some time familiarizing Marty with the various iterations of the game, he invited a group of his friends to come and play. I knew from my own experience that the process of learning the game would be far more compelling if it involved money, if there was something at stake, however little. But given that I was an experienced adult and they were twelve-year-olds, I offered them the following arrangement to try and level the playing field: I would spot each of them five bucks worth of chips; if they lost the five bucks worth of chips, they could walk, free and clear; if they made money, they would get to keep it all, including the initial five bucks; and if they lost but wanted to continue, they would have to put up their own money, at a maximum amount of five bucks. I didn't keep close tabs on the flow of the money, but over the years I think it was pretty much a wash.

The house rules were simple: quarter-dollar, dealer's choice, no cards on the forehead, and the best low is five-four. I favored this over six-four because it would sometimes produce opportunities for going both ways on a straight or a flush or a straight flush. In addition to playing for real money, the kids were attracted by a green felt cloth I draped over the kitchen table, and by good-quality clay chips that had weight and made the sound of real casino chips when tossed into the pot. I taught them that when they were the dealer they should describe the action coming down on the table as they dealt out the cards. A typical narrative might go something like "six of hearts (nice low), jack of spades (in suit), eight of clubs (no apparent help), queen of desmosomes (won't stretch to the seven), four of clubs (pair of fours, paregoric)."

We played a lot of poker and had a lot of fun, but the group needed a name. I had been re-reading Tom Wolfe's *The Right Stuff* and recalled his characterization of test pilots a notch below Chuck Yeager as "pudknockers," and thought this fit my band of soon-to-be teenagers. Despite the pejorative connotation, this moniker became a sought-after badge of honor, combining elements of ineptitude and high accomplishment (not every pilot can fly a fighter jet; not every teenager can play old-time poker—but if you can, that's cool).

The original lineup consisted of Marty "Mart-Dogg" Fitchen, Brent "Brently" Blattner, Matt "Berry" Berry, Douglas "Dougie" Brooks, Erik "E.P." Peterson, Gavin "G-Dub" Wahl-Stephens, and Nick "Nicky" Blattner, with honorable mentions to Matt Fitchen, Nick Chapin, and Cam Hering (who can talk backward—literally). They were and are a grand bunch of lads, full of fun and repartee. During breaks from the poker, we would adjourn to the patio and, in their words, I would "hold court."

During one of these sessions, I regaled them with "profound" tidbits such as the meaning of the word "effete" (how we got on this topic I do not know, but get on it we did, and happily so, as it soon became part of Pudknocker lore). I exhorted them, "Don't you remember Spiro Agnew, the vituperative VP under Richard Nixon from 1969–1973? He bashed the media as 'effete impudent

The Pudknockers grew up, but still play poker. *Left to right*: Erik Peterson, Douglas Brooks, Matt Berry, Nick Blattner, Brent Blattner, Marty Fitchen, and John Fitchen (Gavin Wahl-Stephens in absentia), October 2017

snobs.'" With his characteristic deadpan, Berry labelled this an "only-John-can-use-a-five-syllable-word-to-explain-a-two-syllable-word" pearl of wisdom. The guys were kind enough not to point out that none of them had even been born when Agnew launched his verbal attack.

I confessed that I liked sesquipedalian (multisyllabic) words, but only if they were the right ones—*les mots justes*. To use big words simply because they are long is an exercise in pedantry—one should seek a nuanced vocabulary full of the right words. If there's a short word that says it just right, use it. If there's a long word that says it better, use it.

Here's an example—you be the judge. Is it better to use one really big word

pneumonoultramicroscopicsilicovolcanoconiosis

or a collection of short ones

lung damage caused by breathing
tiny particles of volcanic ash

I know this is over-the-top, but the guys seemed to like it, so I kept on doing it. And in the end, I think they knew my wish was for them to be clear and concise, and I joined them in chuckling at an old man's mental machinations.

At the end of senior year in high school, when the boys prepared to head off to college, our meetings were lubricated by beer and pot (in moderation of course), which made for new adventures in and around the poker table.

One Friday at around midnight, Gavin (the designated driver), Berry (shotgun) and E.P. (in the back), set forth in Gavin's minivan to get donuts at the local 7-11. On the way back, they pulled off at the Crystal Springs Rhododendron Garden to commune with nature. The parking lot at the garden is across the street from the Reed College campus, and is off-limits after dark (though this is rarely enforced). As they pulled in, the college security jeep appeared from behind. Wanting to avoid trouble, Gavin kept the van in gear and lurched toward the exit. Preoccupied by the security vehicle in his rearview mirror, he neglected to look left as he pulled out, and cut off a real cop driving down the street.

With his eyes now fixed on the cruiser behind him, Gavin was shocked out of his trance by Berry, who shouted, "Stop sign! Stop! STOP!" Gavin slammed on the brakes and screeched to a halt. Slowly, cautiously, he started up again, and crept home as the cop tailed the van. When the boys finally turned onto our quiet street, the cop did as well, and then turned on his flashing lights. Gavin pulled to the curb.

Hunched in the back of the van, E.P.'s life flashed before him—"We could be arrested, college is down the drain, my life is ruined!" Berry called Marty—but there was no answer, as it was one in the morning. The cop approached the window.

"Have you boys been drinking?" he asked.

"No sir," intoned Gavin, his voice quavering.

"License and registration," said the cop.

Searching feverishly for his wallet, Gavin couldn't find it.

"Sorry, sir, I don't seem to have it with me."

"I see. What's your driver's license number?" Without hesitation, Gavin recited his seven-digit Oregon license number verbatim. (Nice work, G-Dub.)

After what seemed to the guys like an eternity, Marty finally noticed the cop's lights flashing on our kitchen wall and woke me up. I walked down the driveway in my PJs and robe, feeling calm and confident—probably because I was still half asleep, but also because the boys looked appropriately contrite. Mustering my most respectful tone, I said to the cop, "Officer, these boys are with me."

"Then get these guys to bed. They can walk from here."

From then on I would be viewed as their savior. All I can say is that I will be forever grateful to that cop, who essentially shepherded my guys safely back home. I don't know that we deserved his leniency, but I'm mighty glad he was willing to extend it.

During a subsequent poker game, I stepped out onto the patio for a nighttime listen, and right on cue a Western Screen Owl chimed in with its accelerating series of short whistles, reminiscent of a bouncing ping pong ball. I answered the owl's call and it replied. I hurried inside with a finger to my lips signaling for the boys to be quiet as they followed me back outside. I called again, and to the guys' utter amazement, the owl answered. I asked if they thought they could reproduce the call. Cam volunteered right away and gave forth a perfect rendition. The owl responded, changing its tone to a softer, cooing sound, an appeal, an invitation. Cam cooed back sweetly and the owl swooped down, gently touching the top of Cam's head. As the bird flew off, there was complete silence. In that moment, we felt the connection between humans and nature—an epiphany. To this day, the guys remember fondly that special encounter in my urban backyard.

Over the years, the Pudknockers have stuck together and the poker games have continued. They gave me a handsome wooden chip holder, designated the Pudknockers Saving and Loan because there is always some spare cash in the box as well as a set of really cool chips should a Pudknocker find himself in need of a stake for a spontaneous game. When they started college, I told them the free five bucks of chips would come to an end. Inevitably, of course, what they do now is take all the old man's money. I taught them too well—but I'm cheered to see their progress, on the table and off.

They are a fine bunch of young men for whom I feel a deep and enduring fondness—as they, I think, feel for me. We still struggle to define exactly what it means to be a Pudknocker. Here are some ideas. A Pudknocker is:

> An educable reprobate
> An educated reprobate
> A member of the tribe

These thoughts are helpful but they don't nail it down. With a wink of an eye and more than a little irony in her tone, my wife Ellen comes closest. "Pudknockers," she says, "wear a slightly tainted badge of honor with pride."

My advice to them, abridged and somewhat modified, comes from Rudyard Kipling:

> If you can make one heap of all your winnings
> And risk it on one turn of pitch and toss,
> And lose, and start again at your beginnings
> And never breathe a word about your loss;
> If you can talk with crowds and keep your virtue,
> Or walk with Kings—nor lose the common touch,
> Yours is the Earth and everything that's in it,
> And—which is more—you'll be a Pudknocker, my son.

FIELD NOTES

Seen flying over Columbia River at Broughton Beach from boat ramp to Sea Scout base on 11/18/16. Pointed out to me by David Leal and also seen with Tait Anderson and Beverly Hallburg. Very large compared to associated gulls, roughly two times the size. Unmistakable, massive pelican bill—grayish overall with yellow tinges. wings bowed when gliding into the stiff east wind. Back and leading edge of wing pale gray; trailing edge darker gray.

Bird #295. **Brown Pelican**

[Code-5]

CHAPTER 17
ATTU: THE HOLY GRAIL OF NORTH AMERICAN BIRDING

I wrote this chapter in 2001, a year after returning from Attu. Portions of it appeared in the *Atlantic*, October 2001, and in *Attu: Birding on the Edge*, published by the American Birding Association in 2003. Birding statistics cited in the narrative were current at the time of writing.

We stood huddled on the soggy tundra beside the remote airstrip, our backs to the thirty-five-knot wind and horizontal sleet. Driven by internal engines hard to explain to those we had left behind, we came to this stark and distant place in search of birds. As the sleet pelted Gore-Tex and penetrated cracks in our clothing, I found myself wondering, *Why am I here? Why do we do this?*

Sitting on the tarmac in front of us was the plane that had brought us, a 1950s-vintage Lockheed Electra L-188 turboprop operated by Reeve Aleutian Airways. The Electra looked old-fashioned but seasoned, as well it might since it is a close relative of the planes used by the US Weather Service to fly into hurricanes. The trusty Electra had carried us 1,492 miles west of Anchorage, past the 180th meridian, to the outermost of the Aleutian Islands: to Attu, the holy grail of North American birding.

The location of Attu is not well depicted on most maps. Attu is so far west, so distant from the Alaskan mainland, that it is usually shown in an inset on maps of that state, or perhaps as a speck off the coast of Asia on maps of eastern Siberia. Either way, the key geographical feature of Attu is lost in the presentation. The crucial

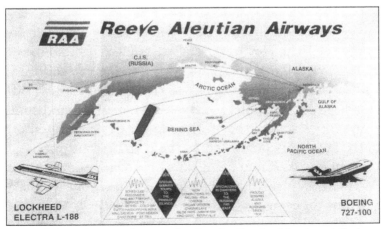

Reeve Aleutian Airways placemat showing the Aleutian Islands and the location of Attu (arrow)—1,492 miles west of Anchorage

fact, at least to birders, is that although the island is part of Alaska, it is much closer to Asia than it is to North America. A surprisingly informative view of the Aleutian geography, of Attu's place in the world, is shown in the route map printed on the paper placemats used by Reeve during in-flight food service.

In bucket-brigade fashion we off-loaded our luggage and a few boxes of supplies from the cargo bay, and stowed them under a tarp at the side of the runway. It was noon ABT (Attu Birding Time). We turned to watch the Electra taxi for takeoff. With a vague sense of foreboding, I realized the plane would not soon return. Like it or not, we were going to spend the next two weeks on this desolate island, uninhabited except for us birders and a handful of US Coast Guard personnel operating a LORAN (Long Range Navigation) station. As we stood shivering by the runway, the leaders explained that they needed some time to get our quarters set up. In the meantime, we were all going birding!

For the next five hours, in what became whimsically known as "The Death March," we trudged around in the general vicinity of the runway and along the shores of Massacre Bay. The weather was so foul that birding was essentially impossible. Eyeglasses, binoculars, and spotting scopes were either fogged up, water-splattered, or both. Finally, we returned to the tarp by the runway to pick up our stuff and lug it the two miles to Lower Base. As I bent into the howling wind and dermabrasive sleet, the thought came again: *Why am I here? Why do we do this?*

Things in Anchorage had not gone smoothly. Plans for an advance party to fly to Attu to lay in provisions and prepare for the arrival of the main body had evaporated when

Reeve encountered a series of equipment problems—most importantly a cracked windshield which had to be replaced with a part flown in from Sweden. As a result, the advance party and main body would have to fly together and our individual luggage weight limit, originally set at forty-five pounds, would be reduced to twelve. A C-130 cargo plane, arranged at the eleventh hour, would fly in the balance of our luggage, as well as food and other supplies. The C-130 would follow a few hours behind the Electra after loading was completed. Given the vagaries of weather and antiquated equipment, this sort of last-minute improvisation was apparently "normal" for trips to Attu.

While we had been on the Death March, the weather had deteriorated, and the C-130, trailing our flight by some three hours, was unable to land. We fretted about the balance of our luggage: the organizers fretted about other things, like food and toilet paper. Backup provisions had been stored in the upper building ("Upper Base," as it was called) at the end of the previous season, but over the winter the building had been broken into by persons unknown. Only a few things had been stolen, most notably some large cans of WD-40, but the door had been left ajar and rats had gained access to the stored food. When the leaders entered the building, there were rats everywhere. One room that previously had been used as sleeping quarters for the leaders and other staff was so badly infested that it had to be sealed off for the duration of our stay. Most of the packaged goods had been devoured by the rats, but apparently some canned goods had survived.

A recent convert to serious birding, I had been unaware of Attu except as a distant battle site in World War II. Then, in September of 1998, while bouncing around in a fishing boat on a pelagic trip off the coast of Monterey, California, I listened intently as one of the guides described his experience on Attu that spring. He spoke with awe and excitement about the unbelievable birds he had seen, about the fact that he had gotten lots of lifers, even though he already had an ABA list of more than 700 species before going on the trip.

When I got home, I tracked down Larry Balch, the director of Attour, Inc., the outfit that had organized birding trips to Attu since the late 1970s. He told me that the trips offered in 2000 would be the last. The Coast Guard station was scheduled to close in the next few years, and when the station closed, there would be no one to maintain the airstrip, the only viable access to the island. I sent in deposits for Ellen and me, for the May 2000 trip—the first of the final year.

Over the ensuing months, as we received a steady stream of information from Attour, Ellen began to waver. There were descriptions of the Attuvian weather and the primitive living conditions; lists of recommended clothing, of footwear appropriate for walking the soggy tundra, and of sources for watertight gloves; admonitions about the remoteness from medical facilities and warnings that fickle weather could delay arrival or postpone departure; exhortations to show up in good shape, as all travel on the island would be by foot or mountain bike on rough terrain, and we would need to move quickly when a good bird was discovered. Ellen is a lover of nature who delights in looking at birds, but she is not obsessed like me. Ultimately, she demurred, reasoning that if she didn't like Attu she couldn't just take the next plane home. And she was right—there is no scheduled commercial air service to the island, so when you're there, you're there until the plane comes to get you two weeks hence … if then.

Now, some eighteen months after I had signed up, here I was (minus my favorite birding companion) in the wind and sleet with a bunch of people I'd never met, all of whom I presumed to be deranged because, like me, they had chosen to come to Attu. There were eighty-six of us in all—sixty-three men and twenty-three women; seventy-four paying customers and twelve leaders/staff. The paying customers had shelled out nearly $5,000 each—not including travel to and from Anchorage—to fly to Attu and spend two weeks living in marginal conditions searching for rare birds on this cold, remote island.

Why is Attu so special, such a storied place in the lore of North American birding? Less than 250 miles from Russia's Commander Islands, and almost 1,500 miles from Anchorage, Attu is still part of the state of Alaska, and therefore part of North America. At the time, this meant that it was also part of the so-called ABA Area, a territory defined by the American Birding Association as North America north of Mexico, excluding the Caribbean, Greenland, and Hawaii. (Hawaii has since been added.) This matters to birders because we keep lists of birds seen in specific geographical regions. For many, the list of birds they have seen in the ABA Area is the most important, a

Lower Base

critical yardstick of their skill and achievement. Because Attu is close to Asia, Asian birds are more likely to show up there than on the North American mainland. And if these Asian birds are seen on Attu, they count as ABA birds. Attu is famous because it delivers Asian birds within the ABA Area—lifers, birds to add to one's life list, birds to build one's ABA total.

As we approached the aging building at the south end of Casco Cove, it was hard to believe that this decrepit structure could possibly house eighty-six people for the coming two weeks. Our "hotel," erected just after World War II, had been abandoned in the 1960s and left unmaintained since. Exhausted, soaked, and curious, we went inside. Despite ongoing mopping and the use of "salamanders"—kerosene-powered fans that blew hot air onto the surface—the concrete floors were soaked throughout the building. In most places, the cement walls were crumbling.

As I walked down the dank hallway and peered into the rooms, I noticed some writing on the few places where the walls were smooth—summaries of previous trips, with names and life totals for the ABA Area. Some of the totals were over 800, and nearly all of the rest were in the 600s and 700s. A few months before departing for Attu, I had taken considerable pride in reaching the 500-bird milestone for the ABA Area. I stared at the big numbers on the wall and thought, *Holy shit, I'd better keep my mouth shut.*

I was assigned to room nine, a twelve-by-eight-foot space that I would share with nine other men. A cardboard sign on the wall, left by the previous year's occupants, read "Home Swamp Home." The room was furnished with five bunk beds. Since all ten of us were essentially middle-aged men, protestations of the need for a lower bunk because of "prostate problems" fell on deaf ears.

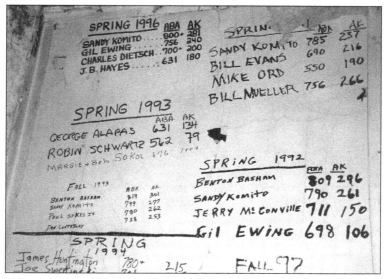

Life totals on a wall at Lower Base

Storage was another problem. Nothing could be left on the floor—it was a quarter inch deep in water—and the concrete walls wouldn't accept nails from which to hang things. Over the years, ingenious but rickety rope-and-wire contraptions had been rigged for drying wet clothes, which dripped onto the wet floor in the room; and out in the hallway there were hooks for heavy stuff like parkas, which dripped onto the wet floor in the hallway. Eventually, we distributed our stuff and got ourselves settled.

That night we were served canned chili with stale crackers. Coming, as it did, after the Death March and our uneasy introduction to base, it was one of the best meals I've ever had. Larry Balch, the Attour director, told us he was hopeful the C-130 would be able to get in the next morning, but the situation was touch-and-go. Meanwhile,

Bob Berman (*left*) and Al Driscoll, "Attu Power and Light"—they could make and fix anything

running water was in place, piped in through rubber hoses from a stream a quarter mile up the mountain behind base. As gas generators and diesel heaters kicked in, there would even be hot water. Old-timers assured us we were in great shape, with far more amenities than they'd had in the early years.

After lights out at eleven—just as the sun was setting almost due north of us—I lay in my bunk trying to determine how many of my roommates were snoring. With sound waves bouncing off the concrete walls, I could be sure of only one thing; there were multiple sources of the sonorous reverberations. Two? Three? Six? Hard to tell. Then I began to perceive that there was a soloist in this nocturnal orchestra, a virtuoso who not only snored with great profundity, but who also spoke in his sleep and evidently suffered from sleep apnea as well. His cadenzas would begin quietly, with an even, almost soothing quality. But gradually, the volume and the tempo would increase, rising into a great crescendo, at the peak of which he would cry out "Oh, my God!" His breathing would then abruptly cease, leaving only the accompaniment of the rest of the orchestra. The first few times I heard this, I was ready to spring from my bunk to check his pulse, but in a minute or two he would take a sudden deep and sighing breath and the solo sequence would start anew.

As I lay awake pondering the social implications of initiating cardiopulmonary resuscitation on a man who had simply paused in the course of his nightly routine, the thought came again, *Why am I here? Why do we do this?*

When you start out, birding is simple. The fundamentals are straightforward. I tell beginners to think about *music, motion,* and *anomaly.* Music, because we often hear birds before we see them. Motion, because our eyes are more likely to notice something that is moving than something that is not. Anomaly, because a motionless bird may stand out in some other way; for example, there shouldn't be a lump on a telephone wire, so if you see a lump on a telephone wire, it's probably a bird. Each of these fundamentals has deeper, richer meanings as well. Really good birders can hear a single "chip" and tell you what bird produced it—or at least provide a short list of two or three possibilities. In fact, a good ear is probably the most prevalent attribute of top birders.

Over time you learn that motion has to do with more than simple movement. It has to do with the *kind* of movement—the frequency and depth of wingbeats, flicking of the tail, bobbing of the head. British birders adopted a term used by RAF plane spotters during World War II—*jizz* (from GISS: "general impression of size and shape")—to describe the overall gestalt of a bird, an impression that is often based on the way it moves. Top birders are able to make amazing identifications at great distances from jizz alone. Anomaly becomes more and more powerful as knowledge increases: gulls don't perch in trees but kites do, so look carefully at a gull-sized white bird perched in a tree—it might be a White-Tailed Kite.

In the morning after oatmeal and canned fruit, we walked in the general vicinity of base. The scores of bicycles, most of which had been left on Attu over the winter, would not be ready for a day or two, another casualty of the aborted early arrival of the advance party. The slow pace of the walking on spongy and uneven tundra was useful for getting a clear picture of the background avifauna of the island, especially for an Attu rookie like me. The more clearly you imprint what is common, the more likely you are to perceive the unusual.

Lapland Longspurs were everywhere. Rock Ptarmigans and Gray-Crowned Rosy Finches were easy to find along Casco Bluff, a couple hundred yards from base. Common Eiders and Ancient Murrelets drifted by in the nearby cove, and Tufted Ducks were located on Pump House Pond, just over the ridge behind base. All of these birds are difficult to find in the lower forty-eight states (Ancient Murrelet and Tufted Duck were lifers for me), but here on Attu they were just part of the standard background. At around noon, we broke to have lunch—canned spaghetti.

Just as we settled in at the long tables, one of the leaders, who had stepped behind the building to relieve his bladder, burst into the dining room. "Eurasian Bullfinch behind Upper Base!" Bowls of spaghetti were abandoned en masse as we all tried to cram through the door at the same time. Walter, the cook, stood by the door with an amused look on his face, watching the stampede with knowing eyes. In the confusion and flurry of questions that followed ("Did it land?" "Exactly where?" "Did it fly?" "Which direction?"), nobody was quite sure what had happened or where the bird had gone.

Apparently, while the leader had stood quietly minding his business, the bright red songbird had dropped in on a gust of wind and landed in the scruffy grass, not fifteen feet from the tip of his nose. As his heart pounded, he considered the options. Should he stay put and keep an eye on the bird, hoping that someone else would venture out behind the building? Or should he alert the rest of us immediately before the bird took off? Either decision was likely to be the subject of endless second-guessing. "How could you just stand there and not let us know?" "How could you leave the scene and lose track of the bird?"

Sweeps of the hillside were organized in an effort to flush the bird. All afternoon we fanned out across the tundra, combing the area downwind from Upper Base. Nothing. The search extended into the next day. It was reasoned that the bird might have moved on to Kingfisher Creek, about two miles down the road along Casco Cove. A massive sweep with more than eighty birders spaced at ten- to twenty-yard intervals inched up the valley defined by the creek. Everyone was there, with the top birders leading the way. This was a much-desired bird, a "Code-5" bird in the parlance of the ABA (Code-1 birds are easy to find; Code-6 birds are extinct). Everyone needed the bullfinch, and everyone wanted to be the hero who rediscovered it. Nothing.

Late that day, as they pedaled home, a handful of lucky souls got a brief fly-over glimpse of the bird near the mouth of Kingfisher Creek. This sighting prompted a whole new round of excitement and sweeps. Nothing. The bullfinch was never seen again.

To understand why people go to Attu, why they subject themselves to the rigors of living in a crumbling, dank, abandoned LORAN station, and of biking and hiking across uneven tundra and treacherous snow banks, it's necessary to understand the phenomenon of "listing." Each year, as a supplement to its flagship publication, *Birding*, the ABA publishes a list report. In this report, birders are given an opportunity to make public the number of birds they have seen in the ABA Area (or their state, or the world). If you send in your name and your numbers, you are a "lister."

Listing means more than just keeping lists—it means that you are willing, even eager, to have the size of your list known publicly. Some birders keep track of life lists, but choose to keep that information private. Even though they do not choose to have their information published, many still scrutinize the ABA supplement and derive satisfaction in discovering that they are "ahead" of birder X or birder Y, and that their life list is longer.

In the most recent supplement, only twenty-three birders had ABA totals of 800 or more. The actual number of birders with ABA totals above 800 is unknown. One veteran of Attu told me that for every birder with 800 who wants to brag about it, there are probably five who don't. But even if that's true, this is an elite group. A report compiled by the US Fish and Wildlife Service indicates that more than 60,000,000 Americans are "watchers of birds." The majority of these people watch birds at backyard feeders, but more than a third of them (23,500,000) watch birds "away from home." Birders with 800 ABA birds occupy a lofty place on a very large pyramid. They have amazing drive and persistence. I asked one of them what he did when he got lifer number 800. He looked me in the eye and said in an even tone, "I started looking for 801."

Why is 800 so hard to achieve? The Official ABA Checklist contains a total of 906 species, each of which is assigned a code from 1 to 6. As I said, Code-1 birds are common; Code-6 birds are extinct. Some 665 birds are designated Code-1 or Code-2, and 12 are Code-6. About 130 are Code-5 (five or fewer recorded sightings in the past century), and the rest are Code-3 (seen every year but requires intensive, specialized searching) or Code-4 (found only occasionally and not expected to be encountered every year). According to the Checklist, Code-1 birds "occur routinely and are easily found" and Code-2 birds are "a bit more difficult to find than are Code-1 birds."

This matter-of-fact language makes it sound as if finding Code-1 and Code-2 birds is simple, but the reality is often much tougher. Consider, for example, my personal quest for the Mountain Quail, a Code-2 bird that, like me, is resident in Oregon. In the five years before Attu, I made twenty trips and drove more than 3,000 miles to appropriate habitat, and had yet to get an unequivocal look at this elusive bird. I concluded that Code-2 birds are indeed "a bit more difficult to find."

Finally, in August 2001, ten Mountain Quail walked calmly out in front of me across a dirt road on Bearbones Mountain in the southern Cascades. And to complete my wish list, six months later I saw three more off Skyline Road within the limits of Multnomah County (home of Portland). Both were key sightings for me, adding to my ABA Area and Multnomah County life lists.

Birders like being outdoors, in touch with the biological world, and informed about living things. But they tend to have a special affinity for avian life that transcends the rest of nature. One day, as we were riding our bikes along the shores of Massacre Bay, an orca appeared close to land.

We stopped and gathered to check it out. A straggler, seeing a focused group, sped to catch up, screeched to a halt in our midst, and blurted out, "What've you got?" We pointed toward the water: "There's an orca close in." He paused to process this information. "Does it have feathers?" he asked. Such is the preoccupation of birders.

By day three, the situation had improved considerably: the bikes were operational, the wind had abated, the temperature was now in the high thirties, and the precipitation had ceased. There were even some brief periods of sunshine. Life on Attu began to take on a natural rhythm. You get up, throw on some clothes, walk the 200 yards to Upper Base, eat breakfast, make your lunch, return to Lower Base to add more layers of clothing, mill around in the "courtyard" discussing the weather and what birds it might bring, check your bike, join up with one of the leaders, and head to the venue you are guessing might have something interesting that day.

Birding on Attu is carried out in a great arc centered on Massacre Bay: to the north is the Gilbert Ridge, a range of mountains hugging the northern shore of the bay, with Alexai Point at its eastern end. To the south is Casco Cove, where base is located, and farther south is Murder Point, a promontory looking out over the open expanse of the Pacific Ocean. The violent place names (Murder Point, Massacre Bay) date to the eighteenth and nineteenth centuries, and refer to Russian fur traders' brutal treatment of native Aleuts, not to the bloody battle of World War II. Along the western side of Massacre Bay are a series of spots known as the Runway Ponds, Puffin Island, Navy Town, Debris Beach, Henderson Marsh, and the Pyramid. Base is near the southern end of the arc—a two-mile walk from Murder Point to the south and a twelve-mile bike ride/walk from the tip of Alexai Point to the north and east.

Groups of ten to fifteen birders fan out around the bay, maintaining contact by radio. If a rarity is sighted at Alexai Point, you hope you aren't at Murder Point, fourteen miles away. But even if you are, the wisdom of the old timers is, *go now*, because if you wait till tomorrow, it will probably be gone.

At the end of one particularly peripatetic day, I called home on the intermittently functional satellite phone and told Ellen, "It's been one of those days. Go here, drag in, get the bird; call goes up, next place, hop on your bike, pedal your guts out, walk through the tundra, get to the next place—whoops!—there's a bird somewhere else, go there, get the bird." After a while, you begin to realize that it's a good idea to stay "central"—that is, to position yourself in a location from which you can make a dash in any direction to get an important bird.

When I'm at home, I rarely eat breakfast, but on Attu, I ate breakfast every day. And when the C-130 finally delivered its goodies, I ate a *big* breakfast every day—cold cereal, oatmeal, scrambled eggs, sausage, fruit, milk, coffee, more cereal. Immediately after breakfast, we would repair to a small Quonset hut just outside Upper Base where we would make lunch to carry into the field. The first few days I was timid, thinking there might not be enough to go around. That changed quickly. By day three, I was filling my lunch bag with two sandwiches, three or four candy bars, two bags of pretzels, cheese, yogurt, cookies. Thus armed, I would basically eat all day in the field, return with appetite for Walter's hearty dinner offering, and then continue to munch on whatever was left in my lunch bag until bedtime. Despite this profligate caloric consumption, I lost twelve pounds during my time on Attu.

The Japanese Army occupied Attu and Kiska in June of 1942. Although the strategic significance of this maneuver was debatable, it tangibly affected American morale. In the wake of the disaster at Pearl Harbor, it was unthinkable for President Roosevelt to accept foreign occupation of American soil. The Japanese garrison on Attu, a force of some 2,650 men, was commanded by Colonel Yasuyo Yamasaki. Unable to cover the whole twenty-by-forty-mile island with this modest complement of troops, he ordered his men to build fortifications on the ridges above Massacre Bay in the south, and Holtz Bay to the north.

On the afternoon of May 11, 1943, American soldiers landed on the beaches of Massacre Bay. Another prong of the attack had come ashore north of Holtz Bay in the middle of the night before. With air and sea superiority and some 16,000 men at their disposal, the US generals believed they could capture the island in a matter of days. They were wrong. The soldiers who manned the invasion had been trained for fighting the desert campaign in Africa, and many were dressed in short-sleeved fatigues.

The battle that ensued, the second bloodiest in the Pacific theater (Okinawa was first), lasted almost three

World War II debris at Barbara Point

weeks and cost 549 American lives, plus over 3,200 wounded. In a secret report, US commanders conceded that "frostbite casualties exceeded battle casualties two to one." The climax came on May 29, when the remaining Japanese, by this time hopelessly outnumbered, mounted a succession of suicide charges against the American positions on the ridges at the head of Massacre Valley. When the battle was over, only 28 Japanese had survived.

Fifty-seven years later, reminders of the Battle of Attu are still strewn across the landscape. Overgrown foxholes dent the high ground, the shore at Barbara Point is clogged with rusting heaps of abandoned materiel, and twisted piles of Marsden matting—used in the war to make roads and runways across the spongy tundra—dot the level portions of the topography. We were cautioned to watch where we stepped, but it's hard to watch your feet when you're looking for birds. Inevitably, a preoccupied birder impaled his big toe on a rusty memento of World War II. Putting pursuit over pain—he was closing in on 700—he biked and hiked over twenty-five miles before returning to base to assess the damage. With eight doctors in the group, there were inevitably eight different opinions on the best way to manage the wound. The only thing we agreed on was that the man needed a tetanus shot. A call was made to the Coast Guard station three miles away, a runner was dispatched, an ampoule of tetanus toxoid was delivered, and the shot was given. Patient and doctors were doing fine.

As the days passed, there was growing concern about the weather. It had become too nice. The wind abated, the rain stopped, and the sun came out. Ultimately, we

Makeshift hot tub built by Attu Power and Light

211

had nine straight days without precipitation—an Attour record. At first this was a welcome change, a chance to dry out and warm up, even to bask in the luxury of a makeshift hot tub. But the respite from bad weather came at a high price, as would become abundantly clear—no new birds. The sentiment shifted from "We need a break" to "We need a storm." We would later be reminded of the aphorism, "Be careful what you wish for."

At fifty-four, I figured I would be one of the oldest people on Attu. Given the pre-trip descriptions of the rigors of life on the island, I thought that most of the participants would be in their twenties or thirties. I couldn't have been more wrong. Most of us were in our fifties or sixties or seventies, and I'm pretty sure we were graced by the presence of an octogenarian or two. On reflection, this makes sense, I suppose, given the duration of the trip: people who have retired would be more likely to have the time, and perhaps the money. The age of the participants was incongruous, however, with the physical demands of birding on Attu—at odds with the hours of walking, the miles of biking, the climbing of snow banks, and the

Fording the Peaceful River

fording of rivers. It was remarkable how fit everyone was, and how game. One woman in her sixties fractured two ribs when she fell from her bike onto a rocky escarpment on the way to Alexai Point. She rested at base for a single day, and then gritted her teeth, climbed back on her bike, and set forth into the field once again.

In the interest of staying central, I was with a group walking the beaches of Casco Cove when the call came in from the Pyramid. Siberian Rubythroat! We piled onto our bikes for the four-mile dash, praying that the bird would stay put. When we arrived, a row of birders was stationed along the rutted track, scopes and binoculars trained on the willow shrubs at the base of the ridge. The bird, they said, was just behind a small rise, and might pop up at any time. I focused my binoculars on the little clump of dwarf willows, staring at a tan leaf that seemed larger than the leaves typical of these small shrubs.

Then, suddenly—*wham!* The "leaf" turned toward me with a dazzling flash of its fiery red throat. Over the course of the next hour, we worked our way to a small embankment above the dwarf willows where the bird was foraging. From this vantage point, we could get nearly continuous looks at the bird through spotting scopes from close range. As I looked down at this extraordinary creature, at this small bird with great impact, a birder behind me spoke in a hushed voice. "Jeeezuss!" he said. "What a bird!"

Birders usually don't say, "I *saw* the bird"—they say "I *got* the bird" or "I *have* the bird." And when they have gotten it, they *take* it (tick it on their life list). The choice of verbs is revealing, suggesting possession, ownership. "Getting," "having," and "taking" harken back to our hunter-gatherer ancestry. But there is deeper level, too. There is a point at which you *know* the bird. The bird is in your brain—you know its form, its behavior, its seasonal timing, its preferred habitat, its silhouette, its call, its song, its jizz. You can identify it at great distance in fading light because *you know that bird.* And what's more, *you know when and where to find it.* The combination of certain identification and reliable location of an unusual bird is highly valuable in the world of birding.

Of course, all birds are not gotten equally. Sometimes the light is perfect, and the bird is close, and lingers, and sings. Sometimes the angle of observation is such that key field marks are readily observed. And then there are times when everything is marginal: the light is poor, the angle is wrong, and the bird is silent, distant, and uncooperative in displaying the necessary parts to the observer. One may *see* a small form flit by, but to *get* it, to know what it is beyond a reasonable doubt—to *have* it, to *take* it—you must see (or hear) specific things: field marks that make the identification solid. Not all the birds on one's life list are perfectly observed. Every serious birder knows that there is "bomb-proof identification" at one end of the spectrum, and "definitely didn't get it" at the other. In between are shades of gray, shades of uncertainty. Where, one might ask, is the threshold and how is it defined?

Certainty of identification is a topic one approaches gingerly, for it may touch a tender nerve—integrity, a birder's value—it may threaten the number, the *life total.* But at some point, all true birders must come to grips with the reality of the identification threshold. How many field marks are enough? How much do you have to see or hear to be certain? When do you *have* the bird? If you are too liberal in ticking life birds, you run the risk of losing the respect of your fellow birders, who may question your integrity—to your face, or worse, behind your back. But if you nitpick, if you insist on seeing every minor detail, and take only those birds that you have seen under ideal conditions, you will cheat yourself out of perfectly acceptable ticks. Where do you draw the line? When do you *have* the bird?

I asked this question of a fellow Attuvian, a retired nephrologist from New Jersey, who told me the key is to get "the essence of the bird." That essence could be a diagnostic field mark, a distinctive call, or jizz. He offered further that he always knew when he had a bird's essence because at that instant he got an adrenaline rush. I asked him how this had been validated. As a diagnostician, a physician-scientist, he stopped to ponder. "You have a point there," he intoned.

The notion of the essence of the bird is right on. I'm still thinking about the adrenaline theory. It has some merit and may be part of why we do what we do.

Another aspect of listing that birders tend not to talk about is *how* one gets a bird. What if you have paid a lot of money to go on a guided tour, the guide finds the bird, frames it in a spotting scope, and then you step up and take a quick look because there are others behind you waiting for their chance? Have you got the bird? Would you know the bird if you encountered it again on your own? Maybe not. Does it still count? For some birders it does, for some it doesn't, and for others it is, well, a shaky lifer, a dubious tick, a "BVD" (better view desired)—a bird with a nagging mental footnote. In the end, the decision to take a bird is an individual choice predicated on a personal honor system with no official referees.

There is a phenomenon that goes beyond listing but is still an integral part of it, a phenomenon that gives full expression to birding mania. In America we call it "chasing." In Britain they call it "twitching." Both terms mean dropping everything to go after a bird you haven't seen before, no matter how distant or difficult to reach. It is a major trend in birding, and an activity that has exploded with the coming of the information age. States and major cities have bird alert hotlines—updated weekly, daily or even hourly—and emails broadcast rarities seen around the world. Information on rare bird sightings can be retrieved instantaneously from birding websites.

When a rare bird shows up somewhere, the word goes out electronically, emails hum, cell phones ring, and chasers make spur-of-the-moment trips to get a bird they may not even have heard of the day before. One of the birders on Attu told me he keeps a separate list, an "NBA" (no bird alert) list. He still checks the hotlines and websites, and searches for the birds they report—but he also wants to keep track of what he has found on his own. A similar concept is being explored by the ABA Recording Standards and Ethics Committee: self-found lists would require "that you only count birds you found yourself, not ones found by others and pointed out to you, or reported on bird alerts."

I'm sitting at Murder Point, hunched against the wind, in

a hole between two hummocks, thinking, *This sea-watch is a waste of time. I don't have a scope with me, and even if I did, the birds the leaders are pointing out to us are near the gloomy margin of the optics—a zone where they are comfortable and confident because of years of local experience, but a zone beyond my personal sense of internally comfortable identification. I need to go somewhere else.* The timing of the radio report is perfect—a Mongolian Plover has just been sighted at the tip of Alexai Point. I'm as far away as I can be, but nothing's happening here, I'm in shape, the old-timers say to go now—don't wait, I need this bird, I'm gonna go for it!

So I fast-walk the two miles to base, climb on my bike and pedal six miles to the beginning of the Gilbert Ridge, then on and off the bike to push it through the snow banks that lie across the track every couple hundred yards for four miles along the ridge, and finally two more miles on foot to arrive at Alexai Point. It has taken me over two hours to travel the fourteen miles from Murder Point to Alexai Point. "Is it still here?" I ask the people at the stakeout, gasping for breath. "Haven't seen it for at least half an hour," they tell me, "but we're about to go out on the tidal rocks—that's where it flew." The kelp on the rocks is wet and slippery, the tide is coming in and we need to hurry before our exit route is submerged.

And then: "Oh my god—there it is!"

With chest heaving, I get great looks at this beautiful bird—a fragile, sweet, innocent being on the kelp and rocks in the middle of this huge expanse. The old-timers are right. Go for it now! This is a special bird, worth the fourteen miles—worth the ruts, and snow, and slippery rocks—worth every bit of effort.

A few months before I left for Attu, a good friend asked me why I was going. He had made the effort to locate Attu in an atlas, and even to read about the role it played in World War II, so I took his question seriously. As my departure for Attu came closer, and as my sense of anticipation grew, I was surprised by the intensity of my excitement and intrigued by what it might reveal about birding and birders, and about me. *Why*, I wondered, *do we do it?* What are the motivations and the rewards, the drivers of our unusual behavior? Why are we willing to pay substantial amounts of money to live in marginal circumstances in order to spend day after day looking for birds? My wonderment was intensified by the reality of being on the island.

The allure was hard to explain, I told my friend, but I'd try. It has to do with the confluence of nature, curiosity, discovery, and satisfaction. Although interesting birds can show up anywhere, they tend to congregate in remote, wild places.

Add to a basic love of nature the extraordinary diversity of avifauna; the subtleties of morphology, behavior, and habitat; the fact that birds brighten our lives with song and color; the joy of an unequivocal sighting after an arduous trek; the realization that chance favors the prepared mind; the shared experiences etched in memory because a certain special bird recalls the time and the place and the people—and you begin to understand what drives birders to go where we go and do what we do.

I asked my questions of some of the people I met

on Attu. Not right away—not before I had a sense of the pecking order, of the personalities, of the relative amplitude of the drive. I had the sense that people were reluctant to talk about their motivations. There was a careful dance, for example, about numbers, life numbers. We didn't ask and we didn't tell. But gradually, through one mechanism or another, the numbers became known.

When I finally did ask "Why?" participants were even more reluctant. Are the reasons too personal? Too self-re-velatory? Never pondered or articulated? I found then, and continue to find, that why we bird is not an easy question to answer, and not a question that birders seem ready to discuss. Maybe they have never thought about it. (Is that possible, given the commitment of time, energy, and money—the complexities of orchestrating and justifying frequent absences from family and career to pursue feathered creatures?) Or maybe there's a sense that talking about it will ruin it—that trying to define the etiology of our passion will somehow trivialize the feelings that fuel it.

One of my favorite people on Attu was honest enough to admit that for her, birding is an obsession, maybe even an addiction. In an effort to explain, she invoked words and phrases like "freedom of flight," "gift of song," "adventure," "stillness," and (my favorite) "it keeps me looking upward." These things speak to the spiritual aspects of birding, but I'm not sure they account for the obsession. One senses there is more. There's something in our guts, something visceral, something so powerful that we speak in terms of obsession, even addiction. And more important than our words are our actions—we do things like going to Attu.

The appeal of birding may have something to do with

feeling "cool," "smart," "sophisticated." We know that in many ways birding is viewed as a nerdy activity—we even go along with this, sort of, making jokes among ourselves about our bizarre behavior, our seemingly absurd preoccupation. But inside we feel cool because beneath the nerdy exterior is a serious intellectual endeavor, a science, a passion attuned with nature. We feel smart—more enlightened than those who walk through the park oblivious to the glories that surround them. We feel sophisticated because we know what it takes: the fund of knowledge, the nimbleness of mind and focus necessary to sort and apply a huge amount of information to arrive at the identification of a bird whose essence may have been no more than a fleeting glimpse. Or better still, we have the moxie to identify a bird we've never seen before because we are prepared. We've studied the books and paid attention in the field. We know the rich texture and the subtle hues of the standard canvas. We've contemplated the possible. And when a rarity occurs, it stands out. *We know what it is and call out its name!* Birders admire this moxie, perhaps above all else.

Another compelling part of birding is competition. Attu was my first real introduction to listing, and in the process of trying to understand that phenomenon, it dawned on me that some people (even I?) might be intensely competitive about this sport. Is it a competitive act, for example, to call out the name of a rare bird while other mere mortal birders stand around you, transfixed by your brilliance and bravado? If you're right, you must be a savvy birder. More than that, you must occupy a lofty place on the ABA pyramid. Imagine if you could preface the bird's name with "First

North American sighting of a ..." That would be the big time! Of course, if you're wrong, well, you don't measure up.

Birders dream of finding something rare or out of place, of making certain identification, and of bringing their discovery to the attention of other birders. There is other evidence of competition that I don't fully understand but I know I don't like—competition that seems to suspend human decorum. Competition that can forget common decency and make otherwise likable humans knock you to the ground in the stampede to get a new bird.

One of my heroes on Attu was a retired furniture designer from New Jersey. He was an elegant man, an intense birder, and a sensitive human being. His proudest achievement as a birder was his New Jersey state list. State lists are revealing because they are more likely to have resulted from personal knowledge and experience than from guided tours. Extensive state lists reflect a profound awareness of a group of birds—of seasons and habitats, of what is regular and what is unusual. He had been to Attu before, and returned with modest but hopeful expectations. To his chagrin, he got only two ABA lifers on Attu, and while he was away from home, what would have been three exceptional state birds showed up in New Jersey. Birding takes persistence and equanimity. He has both.

Another of my Attu heroes was a mail carrier from Iowa. He was inspiring because he was simultaneously a mail carrier, a world-class birder, and a philosopher. He asked me quietly one day as we were sweeping the runway ponds, "So, John, have you gone over to the dark side yet?"

I have pondered the meaning of that question ever since, and I don't yet know the answer.

The storm we had wished for came the day before we were scheduled to leave. In a matter of hours, the weather turned from sunshine and warmth to cold, rain, and eighty-knot crosswinds—too much even for the Electra. Between the high winds and scheduling problems at Reeve, it was uncertain when the Electra would be able to make it back to Attu—one day late? Two? Three? Five? Nobody knew. Worse, the weather was so bad that birding was nearly impossible. Each morning a few intrepid souls would venture forth into the gale, only to return an hour or two later—soaked, shivering, and empty-handed.

Most of us milled around the day room—reading; making jigsaw puzzles; or playing chess, Scrabble, or bridge. As the days crept by, these activities were less and less effective at filling the time. We were restless— anxious about families and jobs, worried about travel connections, running low on prescription medicines, eager to leave. Finally, after five days of waiting out the storm, word came one morning that we should be by the runway with our gear at noon, ready for the one o'clock arrival of the Electra. With the prospect of release, spirits improved, and when, at eleven thirty, a Gray-Tailed Tattler was sighted east of the runway, spirits improved even more. We raced to get the bird before the runway lights went on—once they did, we would be prohibited from coming back across the tarmac to the appointed gathering place.

The plane's landing depended on the ceiling. The wisdom was that if we could see the top of the nearby LORAN tower, the plane could land; if we couldn't, it

222

couldn't. One o'clock came and went. No plane. The clouds thickened, but the top of the radio tower was still visible. Two o'clock. No plane, and the top of the radio tower was now only intermittently visible. Two-thirty. No plane. Then, at two forty-five, someone saw a speck on the eastern horizon. A battery of high-performance optics zoned in on that speck. It was moving. It had wings. The wings weren't flapping. It was a plane! A four-engine turboprop! The Electra!

People from the second group of birders, stuck in Anchorage for the past five days, bounced off the airplane full of excitement and anticipation. Hurried accounts of what we had seen passed up and down the human conveyor as we off-loaded their luggage and on-loaded ours. As it turned out, their excitement was justified. The storm that had pinned us down brought in its wake a spate of fantastic birds, including a first North American record, a Rufous-Tailed Robin. In their first two days on the island, the second group saw more Asian vagrants and rarities than we had seen in our entire nineteen-day stay. Birding on Attu has much to do with the weather. The bad weather that kept the C-130 out blew in good birds. The fine weather that let us warm up and dry out meant no new birds for almost a week. And the horrendous weather that kept us on the island an extra five days was a bonanza for the group that followed.

Birding makes us feel good. It brings about the union of imagination and reality, of expectation and fruition. With study and anticipation, an image of a rare bird forms in our minds—we imagine what it will sound like, look like, move like. Over time, often over many years, we revisit that image, mold it, refine it—we think we are ready. And then one day, all of a sudden, there it is—unexpected despite all the expectation: the bird *happens*—imagination and reality fuse, adrenaline flows, we are alive. Birding is deeply felt and personal. It connects us to nature, and to our inner selves. We are moved by a new bird at our feeder, an old friend appearing at the local park with the coming of spring, a lifer on Attu. Birds keep us looking upward—learning, imagining, feeling.

For example, the day before we finally left the island, the weather eased enough for us to bike to the runway ponds for close looks at Aleutian Terns gathering to stake out breeding territories. As we walked the hummocks around the ponds, one of the leaders thought he heard a Wood Sandpiper, the Eurasian version of our Lesser Yellowlegs and a Code-4 bird. A gray form that flew like a shorebird whizzed over our heads and dropped in behind a small ridge. We sprinted to the ridge, and then crept to the top. After a fleeting look, the bird was gone. "Damn," I thought to myself. "I saw it, but I didn't get it."

Over the course of the next hour the bird was briefly sighted two more times. Then, suddenly, it landed less than a hundred feet away. It was looking right at us, almost as if it knew why we were there. "Sure would be nice if we could see the back," I whispered to no one in particular. The bird turned 180 degrees, revealing its spangled back, sprinkled with white and gold.

"Wish it would give us a side view so we could see the subtle barring on the flanks and lateral aspect of the tail," said another birder. The sandpiper shifted a bit and turned sideways.

"Doesn't it like to bob its tail?" someone asked. The bird bobbed its tail.

"Aren't the wing linings key—paler than in the Green Sandpiper?" The bird shook itself and raised its wings.

"It would be great to hear the call." A soft, rolling *tweadle, tweadle, tweadle* emanated from the bird.

"Isn't the call louder and harsher when the bird is in display flight?" The bird soared into the air repeating its call, loud and sharp.

As the Wood Sandpiper flew out of sight, there was a brief, stunned silence, then the crowd of bedazzled observers erupted into spontaneous applause—a standing ovation on the windswept tundra.

There is a special feeling about Attu—a feeling that you can let it all hang out, unfettered, unabashedly in pursuit of a collective grand passion, with no need to explain or apologize. Birding on Attu is magical, in part because of the extraordinary birds and in part because of Attu itself. When I returned to civilization I told Ellen that life didn't seem complete without searching for rare birds in great sweeps across treeless Aleutian tundra peppered with hummocks, pitfalls, and the rusting relics of a distant war.

Attu touches the soul.

Wood Sandpiper (photo by Jim Burns)

FIELD NOTES

A small- to medium-sized owl seen at Broughton Beach with Iain and Stites on 12/19/16. Mostly flying/flushing but also perched on rocks. Sandy/tawny overall with smooth wingbeats, white eyebrows. Chin not well seen. Reads much bigger than 9.5-inch length reported by Sibley. Rounded big wings and double the weight of a robin are more consistent with larger presence of the bird.

Bird #296.
Burrowing Owl
[Code-5]

CHAPTER 18

A BIG YEAR IN MULTNOMAH COUNTY

We stood barefoot in the middle of Phalarope Pond, mud oozing between our toes. I looked at Iain and laughed: "If you'd told me in January we'd be slogging through knee-deep mud in August, I'd have said you were out of your mind." Our dogs, Lucy and Bones, bounded ahead, clearly more in their element than were their masters. We squished along behind the dogs, hoping to encounter something unusual. We didn't.

We were in our "Big Year"—a birding term for an all-out effort to see as many species as possible within a defined geographical area in a calendar year. The reality of Big Year birding is that there are many more days *without* new birds than days with them, especially as the year wears on. But going into the heart of the habitat, as we did that day in August and throughout the year, had a lot to do with breaking the Multnomah County Big Year record.

GETTING STARTED

The idea was hatched in early December 2001 when I drove down to Eugene to check out the Black-throated Green Warbler that lingered there for a week or so after being discovered. While waiting for the warbler, I met Don DeWitt, an unassuming guy and fine birder who had set a new Big Year record for Lane County (which includes Eugene) in 2000. He spoke with quiet enthusiasm about the joys and challenges of a Big Year effort.

A few weeks later on the Portland Christmas Bird Count I happened to be assigned to a group led by Iain Tomlinson, a young British birder who had moved to Portland in the spring of 2001. On that day we talked about my encounter with Don DeWitt and then about the idea of teaming up for an attempt at the Big Year record for Multnomah County in 2002. We were an odd pair: a fifty-six-year-old presbyopic professor and a thirty-year-old balding Brit. But we both had plenty of time to devote to the effort: I was on an extended sabbatical and Iain worked nights at a foster care facility. This meant we had all day every day to bird—provided of course that Iain did without certain luxuries, mainly sleep. We figured we would start out quietly (no public pronouncements or grandiose predictions), see how it went for a month or two, and then make a full commitment if the numbers looked good. We agreed it would be a cooperative effort—we would share all sightings and other pertinent information—but our respective individual lists would stand alone. Thus began what proved to be an extraordinary year of great birds and friendly competition.

We did some homework. We learned that the existing Big Year record for Multnomah County was 200 species, set in 1988 by Joe Evanich, author of *A Birder's Guide to Oregon*. We obtained a copy of a Multnomah County checklist prepared by Steve Summers and Craig Miller and published by Oregon Field Ornithologists in 1993. The list was particularly helpful because it contained all the species ever recorded in the county (as of 1993) and assigned a "degree-of-difficulty" code to each bird. The scheme, similar to that adopted by the American Birding Association, was as follows:

Code-1   Nearly always detected with minimal effort

Code-2   Infrequently to often detected, and usually requiring some special effort

Code-3   Scarce and hard to find, and usually requiring intensive, specialized searching

Code-4   Only occasionally found and not expected to occur every year

Code-5   Species that are recorded five or fewer times

We pored over the checklist and the codes and realized that breaking Evanich's record would take some doing. The breakdown of the Summers/Miller checklist for Multnomah County is 109 Code-1s, 56 Code-2s, 22 Code-3s, 44 Code-4s and 68 Code-5s. Even if we got all the Code-1s, 2s, and 3s, it would mean a total of only 187 birds. Clearly we would need to find some rarities.

Although the checklist was published in 1993 and the code assignments don't always reflect what seems to be the current reality, this document proved to be remarkably accurate and highly useful in helping us plan outings and concentrate on potential target birds. It was also the source of animated discussions on how a Big Year in one county might be mathematically compared to a Big Year

Headed west on I-84 at the county line near Bonneville Dam

in another. We never arrived at the perfect formula but were convinced it must involve advanced algebra or differential calculus.

At 435 square miles, Multnomah is the smallest of Oregon's thirty-six counties. For comparison, Harney (10,135 sq mi) is the largest, and Lane (4,554 sq mi) is about in the middle. Multnomah County (or "Mult" as we came to call it) is shaped roughly like a fifty-by-eight-mile rectangle with a concave top and an upper-left extension. It stretches from just above Bonneville Dam on the east to approximately Skyline Drive at the ridge of the West Hills. Its northern boundary is defined by the Columbia River and its southern limit is a more or less straight line cutting across the Willamette River a bit south of the Sellwood Bridge. The upper-left extension consists of the southern half of Sauvie Island—an indication that the visionary founding fathers contemplated the needs of county birders when they drew the lines.

PICKING GOOD PARTNERS

Early on, Iain and I discovered that in addition to a love of birds and birding, we had many other interests in common: science, world geography, the English language (both versions—his and mine), family life, politics, medicine, and current events, to name a few. During the year we talked a lot about birds, birding, and strategy, but dialogue on non-birding topics was an important source of relief during the long dry spells that are certain to occur in the course of a Big Year. In addition to all the common ground, we also found, inevitably, that each of

With Iain (*left*) by the Columbia River, with Sweet Pea, Bones, and Lucy (photo by David Mandell)

us had certain annoying quirks. For example, one of us (who shall go nameless) often confused left and right, and the other (who shall also go nameless) sometimes jumbled avian nomenclature. So a call like "Northern Rough-winged Hawk left of the tall tree on the right, flying right to left," could present a challenge in the field. We learned to look both ways and to apply simultaneous translation to unusual bird names.

If you have a dog, our advice is to include it in the Big Year experience, especially if you are married (and I don't mean married to the dog). We started the year with two dogs (Lucy Fitchen, a seven-year-old black lab, and Bones Tomlinson, a six-year-old border collie/lab mix) and ended it with three—Lucy and Bones plus Sweet Pea Tomlinson, an injured and near-death stray discovered by us on the mud flats at Vanport Wetlands and rescued by soft-touch Barb Tomlinson. Most of the time the effect of the dogs on the birding was neutral to negative— they weren't allowed in certain parks, they flushed birds prematurely, and they'd bump into the tripod at inop-portune moments—but their inclusion had a crucial and overriding positive effect, which was that our wives were favorably inclined towards our daily outings because they could see that the dogs were happy, healthy, trim, and fit. And as the year progressed, they could see that we were all those things, too.

By the end of the year we were indeed both fit—we had walked over 1,200 miles each—but along the way there was some age-related disparity. Take, for example, the Rock Wren we sighted on Larch Mountain. Two messages posted to the Oregon Birders Online (OBOL) mailing list tell the tale:

Subj: Mult. Rock Wren
Date: 6/14/02
From: Iain Tomlinson
To: obol@lists.orst.edu

From the peak of Larch Mtn. John Fitchen and I heard a distant Rock Wren on the snow patch to the north (and about 700' below). It was a tough-ish hike down to the snow patch (it's easier to hike down from the col between the parking area and the peak). At the snow patch we were able to see the bird and enjoy its singing.

Subj: Re: Mult. Rock Wren
Date: 6/14/02
From: John Fitchen
To: obol@lists.orst.edu

To any would-be chasers of the ROCK WREN reported earlier today by Iain "The Mountain Goat" Tomlinson—a word to the wise. What Iain off-handedly calls a "tough-ish hike down" could be roughly translated into American English as a death-defying sixty-degree bushwhack over mushy snow, loose scree, and fallen tree trunks. The whole way down I kept thinking, *Even if the bird is there, we've got to get back up this sucker.* An alternative approach would be to take the trail to the top of the mountain, listen for the song, and hope to get on it with a very powerful scope. The bird was doing a lot of bobbing—a mannerism that might help nail the ID even from a considerable distance.

TOOLS OF THE TRADE

Optics: We each have good binoculars (John: Swarovski EL 8.5 x 42; Iain: Kowa 8 x 45) and pedestrian scopes (John: Swift Panther 22 x 60; Iain: Bushnell Spacemaster 22 x 60 with the handle broken off). We traveled with both scopes in the car, but generally took Iain's into the field because it has a better tripod and he was willing to carry it. One blustery day in December we deployed both scopes to study an enormous flock of blackbirds at Kruger's Farm on Sauvie Island. Four hours and two stiff necks later, we had been rewarded with a blackbird sweep—Rusty, Tricolored, Yellow-headed, Red-winged, and Brewer's—all five species in the same flock in a single morning.

Transportation: At first we were polite and proper about alternating cars, but it soon became evident that it was much more efficient to have a single dedicated vehicle. Over the course of the year we progressively refined our notion of the "well-appointed birdmobile." It was stocked with books, maps, foul-weather gear, extra lens cloths, towels to wipe paw-prints off the seats, toilet paper, a fifty-pound bag of birdseed, tapes, tape player, shrub clippers, and ultimately a machete we discovered at the side of Reeder Road on Sauvie Island. Thus equipped, we were ready to go anywhere, anytime, on a moment's notice.

Electronics: This was 2002, and neither of us owned a cell phone. We commandeered a pair of hand-held walkie-talkies from my son Marty, but forgot to replace the batteries, and so the devices lay silent in the glove compartment the entire year. There was at least one occasion when they would have been useful, at least in allaying anxiety. We were working the grass fields east of the Sandy River Delta for songbirds and raptors. Iain said he wanted to check the power line for Eastern Kingbird and set off across the deep grass. I would follow the road and catch him up in due course.

No sooner had he gone around the bend and out of sight than an Eastern Kingbird showed up perched on a sapling stake, not a hundred feet from me. It was fruitless to yell or whistle—Iain was well out of earshot. *Damn*, I thought. *I wish we'd brought those walkie-talkies.* It turned out that almost simultaneously Iain had found another Eastern Kingbird along the power line. For a good half hour we each stayed put, rooted by indecision, wondering if it was better to keep on the bird, or to go and get the other guy. Finally, Iain's bird flew off. As he came around the corner I started waving frantically to him and pointing at the kingbird. He waved back and pointed toward the power lines. In the end, all was well and the walkie-talkies weren't needed.

References: We carried four books with us at all times in the birdmobile: the Sibley *Guide to Birds*; the *National Geographic Society Field Guide to the Birds of North America*; *Birds of Oregon* by Jeff Gilligan, Mark Smith, Dennis Rogers, and Alan Contreras; and *Shorebirds of the Pacific Northwest* by Dennis Paulson. In addition, we always had with us the Summers/Miller checklist for Multnomah County, complete with difficulty code assignments.

OBOL (Oregon Birders Online): With some notable exceptions—Gray Flycatcher (new since '93), American Redstart [5], Prairie Falcon [5], Say's Phoebe [4], Northern Mockingbird [4], and Lewis's Woodpecker [4]—OBOL was relatively non-productive in getting us on specific birds. In the beginning we regularly chased birds posted on OBOL, but found more often than not that we wasted time doing this because the bird would be gone by the time we arrived—usually the next day, as we wouldn't see postings until we returned from the day's birding. Cell phones would have helped resolve this problem. Worse, we might perseverate on a posted bird for several days without finding it and lose more time in the process.

On the other hand, OBOL (and to a lesser extent, "Tweeters," the Washington version of OBOL) was highly useful in giving us a sense of what was happening outside the county. This raised our collective awareness and helped us concentrate on certain types of habitat, hoping that birds seen elsewhere would show up in Mult. It also gave us ready access to birders around the state, from whom we could get insight and advice on where and when to look for hard-to-find species. And OBOL served an important function as a filter for the certainty of identification. If we were sure enough to post an ID on OBOL (and risk the condemnation of members if we turned out to be wrong), we were sure enough to take the tick. Sometimes, too, our postings meant that other birders would see "our" bird, giving us an external check on what we had found.

BREAKS IN THE ACTION

We each spent about six weeks out of the county during the year—evidence, we hoped, of a modicum of sanity. Iain traveled in the Philippines for five weeks from the end of February through the end of March (there, he saw 324 species, 166 world lifers). He took a few weekend trips as well.

When he was in the Philippines, he sent me an update from an internet café: "Trip going well. 143 lifers so far. Worried a bit about 'two-step' cobras—so-named because that's how far you get when they bite you. I've been told to watch where I step, but I don't want to turn on my flash-light and scare off the owls."

I spent a week in Texas at the end of April (149 species, 13 ABA lifers), two-and-a-half weeks in France in mid-September (lots of good food and wine; 63 species, 25 world lifers), and a week in the Southern California desert in November (lots of golf; one lifer). Travel in March proved to be good timing—all species missed by Iain during the month were "recouped" within 10 days of his return. Travel in April and September was more costly—three Code-4 and -5 species seen during those timeframes—Dusky Flycatcher [4], White-Tailed Kite [4], American Redstart [5]—never reappeared. We joked about being "punished" for time outside the county.

There was another form of break in the action that wasn't much fun—the dreaded dry spell. The record drought was endured by Iain. Following the Snow Bunting [5] we saw near the Troutdale Aluminum Plant on November 6, he slogged through twenty-six straight days without a new bird. I was fortunate to fill in a few previous misses (Western Gull [2] and Rough-legged Hawk [2]) during this hiatus, but it was still a drag. Then, in the beginning of December, the floodgates opened: in a mere seven days we got Ross's Goose [4], Blue Jay [5], Rusty Blackbird [5], and Tricolored Blackbird [3]. Big Years are like that: when things are happening, you think there is no limit to what you can accomplish—then it goes quiet and you think you are certifiably crazy.

NUMBERS AND DETAILS

- **Miles driven:** Around 15,000
- **Traffic citations:** 1
- **Miles walked:** At least 1,200 each
- **Serious injuries:** None
- **Time in the field:** At least 2,500 man-hours
- **Bird # 201 (date):**
  - Iain: Gray Jay (August 5)
  - John: Parasitic Jaeger (September 25)
- **Big Year totals:**
  - Iain: 225
  - John: 218
  - Combined: 227
- **Birds seen by Iain only:** Glaucous Gull [2], Northern Saw-Whet Owl [2], Red-Necked Grebe [3], White-Tailed Kite [4], Northern Goshawk [4], Dusky Flycatcher [4], Swainson's Hawk [5], American Redstart [5], Gray Flycatcher (new since '93)
- **Birds seen by John only:** Golden Eagle [4], Northern Mockingbird [4]
- **Breakdown by Codes (combined total):**
  - **Code-1:** 109/109 (100%)
  - **Code-2:** 55/56 (98%) One miss: Mountain Chickadee
  - **Code-3:** 18/22 (82%) Four misses: Clark's Grebe, Acorn Woodpecker, Clark's Nutcracker and Yellow-Breasted Chat
  - **Code-4:** 27/44 (61%)
  - **Code-5:** 18/68 (26%)

- – **Total:** 227/299 (76%). As of July 2018, total recorded species in Mult stands at about 325

- **Birds reported by others but missed by us:** Rose-Breasted Grosbeak (new since '93), Burrowing Owl [5], Whimbrel [5], Clay-Colored Sparrow [5], Brewer's Sparrow [4]. Each of these birds was seen once, reported on OBOL, and not relocated. Would that we had been quicker

- **Birds seen by us but not counted:** Monk Parakeet, Northern Bobwhite, Chukar, Eurasian Green-Winged Teal (the first three birds are introduced species and the teal is recognized only as a subspecies)

HOMAGE TO JOE EVANICH

When Joe Evanich set the Multnomah County Big Year record in 1988, he had to overcome big hurdles. First and foremost, he had no car (apparently by choice). This was almost unimaginable to Iain and me—the birdmobile was a central and critical part of our Big Year effort. With it, we could go almost anywhere, any time, and have at our disposal whatever stuff we might need. Without it, we would have been dead in the water.

Second, Joe did not have the benefit of OBOL. As I've said, OBOL wasn't the crucial factor in finding most birds, but it was clearly helpful in giving us a sense of what to be alert for, and in getting us in touch with other birders. We understand that back in 1988 there was an informal telephone network, but it can't have had the immediacy and reach of a digital mailing list.

Finally, Joe was beginning to develop clinical

manifestations of AIDS, some of which required hospitalization—thereby compromising the time available for birding, and undoubtedly taxing his physical endurance and mental resolve. We were amazed at what he accomplished.

Joe died on his birthday: June 14, 1993. He was only thirty-three. Although neither of us ever met him, we felt connected to him through the experience of Big Year birding in Multnomah County. It would be neat if we could sit down with him and compare lists, exchange ideas, swap "best bird" stories. We're certain he knew the county at least as well as we do.

LESSONS AND REWARDS

As we reflect on the extraordinary experience of our county Big Year, a number of lessons reinforced or learned *de novo* come to mind:

There is no substitute for time in the field. We found a number of key birds simply because we were constantly in the field. We were out there and a great bird would just happen; e.g., the Long-Billed Curlew [5] (second county record) that dropped in as if by magic near 185th and Marine Drive on May 2, and stayed for less than an hour. It was an incredibly lucky sighting, and alas, one that is unlikely to be repeated—this site has since been bulldozed and developed.

Imagine the possible—chance favors the prepared mind. Think about the season, the weather, the habitat, and what might show up; e.g., the Mountain Bluebird [5] that suddenly appeared at the summit of Larch Mountain on July 24, a sunny summer day with easterly winds. The bluebird wasn't our number one target that day, but it was on the list. When it showed up, it was an expected surprise.

Stay informed. Read books and periodicals, talk to other birders, and to non-birders (like fish hatchery workers). Find out what they've been seeing and let them know what you're looking for; e.g., the Harlequin Duck [4] we got because we talked to and then stayed in touch with Matt Brazza of the Eagle Creek Fish Hatchery. He had seen Harlies there the previous fall, and even had a picture of one—and he was kind enough to call us when the birds showed up again.

Try to find another birder with whom to tackle the Big Year. You'll learn more and see more collectively than you would singly, and you'll get out more if there is peer pressure to go; e.g., the Swamp Sparrow [3] we found at Ramsey Lake on December 13—which was a rainy, misty, "I'd rather sleep in" kind of morning.

Focus on Code-3 and -4 birds and have multiple targets for each habitat/outing. The Code-1s and 2s will take care of them-selves, and the 5s will happen when they happen; e.g., the Emperor Goose [5] we found at Coon Point on October 14 while searching goose flocks for Brant [4] and Ross's Goose [4].

Find your own birds. OBOL and other birders can help you find birds, but the real payoff comes when you begin to feel the rhythm of the county on your own; e.g., the Snow Bunting [5] that materialized on the edge of the Columbia River at the Troutdale Aluminum Plant on November 6. On the drive to the site we had talked about reports of buntings elsewhere in the state, and how it felt like it was time for one to show up in Mult.

Go into *the habitat*. Sure, it's useful to stop and scan at the edges, but you'll find more if you get into the thick of it and get some mud between your toes; e.g., the Parasitic Jaeger [4] we observed on September 25 chasing gulls over the mud flats at Sturgeon Lake on Sauvie Island. Had we stayed up on the dike with our shoes on, we would never have seen this bird.

What's cool about county birding is that you come to realize what birds are rare in your own patch, and when you see them, you look with great care. Almost every one of these birds you have seen before outside the county—maybe even in abundance. But seeing a common bird in a place where it is rare forces you to look at it critically—to study it, and to be *sure*. That's a special learning experience that far exceeds a three-second look at a rarity framed in a scope by somebody else.

The rewards of a county Big Year are remarkable. There is inherent pleasure in focusing on a manageable set of birds and a geographical region that you come to know in precise detail. Thanks to the Big Year experience, we can tell you within a meter or two where Multnomah County begins and ends; we can tell you what birds to expect in a given month

Parasitic Jaeger, Multnomah County Big Year bird #201 for John (drawing by Matt Fitchen)

and where you're most likely to find them; we can direct you to nooks and crannies that are good for shorebirds, or divers, or raptors, or rails; and now, more often than not, we can name the bird that is singing. Add to this the thrill of finding and identifying a rarity on your own, and there is a sense of satisfaction that has little to do with breaking records. It approaches pure joy.

A PLUG FOR COUNTY BIRDING

I've spent a lot of time watching birds in Multnomah County. It has been fun and it has paid dividends of many kinds. Most important, it has made me a better birder. I recommend county birding for building skills, knowledge, and confidence. Here are some reasons why:

Affordable: Compared to world birding, ABA birding, or even state birding, county birding is cheap. Air travel is not a factor, driving distances are relatively modest, and overnight lodging is generally not required.

Eco-friendly: Because of the shorter distances, there is less fuel consumed in county birding. And as you get to know your local area, you are more likely to care about protecting it from the threat of ill-advised development or other detrimental impacts.

Manageable: The number of birds you need to learn in a county is significantly less than in a state, a continent, or a planet. This means you have the chance to master a set of birds, to know their field marks, their songs and calls, their timing, their preferred habitat, their jizz. Over time, you come to know them, and you begin to call out their names. And then, one day, you call out their names *in the presence of others.*

Egalitarian: Because county birding is both affordable

and manageable, it is a relatively level playing field. Almost any birder—even those with modest means or aging eyes and ears—can build a substantial county list. It takes time, desire, commitment, and persistence, but it is something almost all of us can do.

Rewarding: The rewards of county birding are much like the rewards of birding in general. But the odds are better. There is a special feeling about knowing your own patch—where to go, what to look for, the other birders likely to show up if a rarity is sighted. There is a certain satisfaction, a comfort almost, in knowing the tapestry of birds and birders who reside and visit. Over time, there comes to be a sense of community and confidence. And if you're serious and persistent, you have a chance of finding a rare bird never before recorded in your county.

Many thanks to all the people who contributed knowledge, information, advice, and support to our effort. I am especially grateful to Don DeWitt, Harry Nehls, Wink Gross, Bob Stites, David Mandell, Pamela Johnston, Paul Sullivan, Tom Love, Jeff Gilligan, Gerard Lillie, James Davis, Dave Helzer, David Bailey, Dave Irons, Donna Lusthoff, and Mr. and Mrs. Joe Evanich, Sr.; to Denise Rennis and Carrie Stevenson of the Port of Portland; to Matt Brazza of the Eagle Creek Fish Hatchery; and to Ellen Fitchen and Barb Tomlinson, of the department of homeland security.

FIELD NOTES

A striking warbler coming to the feeders at the home of Bob and Wendy Burley in NW Portland, seen with Ellen, Bob Stites, and Nels Nelson on 9/5/17. Close views at a birdbath just off their deck. A stunning female warbler in yellow, gray and white. Large black eye in bright yellow head. Dazzling yellow throat and breast. Lower back warm gray. Lower belly and undertail coverts white. Thin dark bill.

Bird #297.
Prothonotary Warbler
[Mult First Record; Code-5]

CHAPTER 19

TWO SPECIAL FRIENDS

I've made a lot of speeches in my life—usually to classrooms full of medical students, professional society meetings, FDA panels, grand rounds, and the like. But speeches and writings of a more personal nature have come along as well, and they remain in my mind and in my heart. Sadly, I have been asked to speak or write about two exceptionally fine men who graced my life and died too young.

Barry Bell was the director of the Portland VA Medical Center from 1985 to 1995 and, as such, was my boss when I was appointed associate chief of staff for research in 1985. Simply put, he was the best boss I ever had. His style was reminiscent of what Tom Peters, in his book *In Search of*

Excellence, called "simultaneously loose/tight management." Early in our relationship, Barry established broad boundaries within which I could operate freely, without specific permission. If I felt I was pushing up against a boundary, I would discuss the issue with him before proceeding. It was an especially fun and exciting time because we inherited a brand-new facility with 478 beds and a separate building devoted to biomedical research.

In addition to his prowess as an honest and respected leader (at thirty-seven, Barry was the youngest hospital director in the VA system—first in Puerto Rico, then Philadelphia, then Portland), he was a man of many extra-curricular interests: history, opera, photography, flying small planes, sailing, bicycling, marathon running, skiing, scuba diving, and bread making. All of this and more while building one of the most successful operations in the VA hospital system.

Barry died on April 24, 2006, of complications of multiple myeloma and a bone marrow transplant. I was honored to speak at a memorial service for him two weeks later at the medical center. Here's what I said:

> Hello, everyone. I'm John Fitchen. I was the ACOS for research from 1985 to 1990, during Barry's early years as medical center director. When I heard that he was planning to undergo another bone marrow transplant, I sent him a note recalling the story he'd told me about being stranded at 17,000 feet on Denali, hunkered down for five days in the middle of a howling blizzard. He dismissed the ordeal with characteristic understatement—"endurance is my long suit," he said. Now he was facing a challenge even tougher than Denali.

"Each hill has its own way of scaling," he wrote me. "Instead of rock and snow I now stand on love and good thoughts."

I went to see him. As always, I was struck by his presence. He had rearranged his bed in the Intensive Care Unit so he could sit beside it, not in it, with laptop, DVD player, and cell phone carefully positioned on the bed and ready for action. Who besides Barry Bell could turn an ICU bed into a desk?

The next day, he sent me an email. "If the outcome of this transplant is not as we hope, I will know from the outpouring of friendship I have received from many friends that the memory people had of me was mostly positive."

I wrote back: "Barry, my memory of you isn't *mostly* positive, it's *all* positive. The real question is this: if it gets too hard to survive this transplant, will you be able to let go? Letting go takes big courage, too."

"I've contemplated that," he replied, "but decided it can only be handled as the facts roll out. I am no martyr, nor am I trying to show others how to do it— only a guy who still wants to live."

Barry Bell was—and is—a potent human being. I feel his spirit today, just as I did twenty years ago, and as I will for the rest of my life. Barry, you are in our thoughts, and softly.

Robert M. "Bob" Wilson, MD, was my best friend. Our life paths were remarkably collinear. We both grew up in college towns—he in Amherst, MA, home of Amherst College, and I in Hamilton, NY, home of Colgate University. Our fathers worked at their respective institutions, his father as the head basketball coach at Amherst and mine as professor of fine arts at Colgate. Bob and I both went to Amherst College, where he was three years ahead of me (I was class of '67, he was class of '64). After Amherst, we both went to the University of Rochester School of Medicine, where he did an extra year in diabetes research, in the lab of Dr. Bill Peck. He became known as "Peck's Bad Boy." The story behind this moniker was unknown to me, but he was, indeed, a bit of a rogue. During our respective stints at Rochester, we crossed paths frequently, especially at the Bungalow, a watering hole proximate to the medical center and frequented by students from the school of nursing—fertile ground for cultivating evanescent relationships. Bob appeared to have a high success rate at this activity. Of course, he was an upperclassman and I a mere fledgling, so our interactions were cordial but superficial.

Fast forward to 1977, Los Angeles. After training at Vermont and Temple, Bob had been appointed assistant professor in the UCLA Department of Medicine where I was completing a fellowship in the division of hematology and medical oncology. One day I was walking down a hospital ward and heard someone shout, "Fitchen! What the hell are you doing here?" It turned out that his office was a hundred feet from mine—and from then on we saw each other at work at least daily, often on weekends (LA traffic notwithstanding—he and wife Judy lived in the Valley, and Ellen and I lived in the Wilshire District near Hollywood), and regularly on vacations. Our discussions were wide-ranging and stimulating: sports, philosophy, politics (governmental, academic, medical), women in medicine, women in general, and the advent of computers in medical practice, to name a few.

Bob had a timeshare in Palm Desert. Each year we would spend a week batching it—playing golf, drinking scotch, and soaking up the rays. He was a better golfer than I (my first shot of the round typically landed on the rooftops of the houses that lined the right side of the first hole) which resulted in endless kibitzing on how many strokes I should be spotted to level the playing field. When, in 1981, I moved to Oregon and he moved to Vermont, we still spoke on the phone almost daily, and the annual timeshare tradition carried on for nearly thirty years. It was clearly special for both of us.

When he died suddenly and unexpectedly in February of 2007, I wrote an *In Memoriam* piece for the *Amherst Magazine*. Here's what it said:

> Dr. Bob Wilson died suddenly on February 7, 2007, of an acute myocardial infarction after a glorious day of skiing in Crested Butte, Colorado. His wife Judy (Smith '64) was at his side.
>
> Bob was a complex and endearing human being, a contrarian who enlivened conversation with surprising and provocative interjections aimed more, I suspect, at enriching the dialogue than at pushing a particular point of view. Broadly interested and well informed, he respected people from all walks of life. And like all of us, he was flawed. The beauty of Bob was that he was *admittedly* flawed, and because of that he was tolerant of the foibles of others. He was the kind of guy who, sensing your need for counsel or comfort, would

answer the phone at four in the morning and be an ear till the sun came up, occasionally asking a quiet question to let you know he was still listening.

After med school at the University of Rochester and training at Vermont and Temple, he joined the medical faculty at UCLA in 1977. Four years later, he and Judy made a life-changing decision. They left the throb of the city, the vicissitudes of academic life, the chance for fame and fortune, to seek a more cohesive community and proximity to the great outdoors. Bob joined the Mt. Ascutney Medical Group in Windsor, Vermont, where he would practice general internal medicine for the next twenty-four years.

He was an exceptional physician with the perfect balance of knowledge, experience and compassion— the essential ingredients of what we doctors call "good clinical judgment." He listened carefully to his patients; he knew when to act and when to wait, how to make decisions based on imperfect information, when to push and how hard. Despite the fact that we were separated by 3,000 miles, he was the one I always called first and his was the opinion I always trusted most when it came to my own health and that of my family.

Sports were part of Bob's life from birth. He grew up in Amherst where his father, Rick Wilson, was the basketball coach at the college for twenty-nine years. Perhaps because he was a coach's son, Bob was both a participant in sports and a student of sports. He was also a tenacious competitor. When he was quarterback and captain of the Amherst High School football team, he took a wicked blow to the head in a critical game. He picked himself up, stumbled to the huddle and called the play. "Twelve on two." Six downs later, when he had called "Twelve on two" six plays in a row, it dawned on his teammates that something was amiss. Bob was so determined to win that they had to drag him off the field.

At the age of fifty-six, he made another gutsy move, putting his practice on hold for a year while he completed a sports medicine fellowship at Marshall University in Huntington, West Virginia. It added a new and welcome dimension to his career, and it consolidated his love of medicine with his love of sports. He was a volunteer teacher at Dartmouth Medical School and received standing ovations for talks with titles like "Physical Examination of the Human Knee." When he retired in 2005, he relished the opportunity

Leaning in with Bob Wilson (*left*) (photo by Judy Wilson)

it afforded for new learning, travel, and, his greatest joy, time spent with his grandchildren.

He was an extraordinary solver of puzzles. He routinely did standard crossword puzzles without the grid. But his full virtuosity came forth in solving cryptic puzzles like the ones published by *The Atlantic* and *Harper's*. I'd call him up and say, "I'm stuck on the clue that reads: 'A racer at the front, in problem-solving course, running epic race.'" And he'd say, "Oh, let's see … 'A racer at the front' is *ar*, 'problem-solving course' is *math*, so we've got *ar* in *math* or *marath*, 'running' means *on* so we add *on* to *marath* and we have *marathon* which happens to mean 'epic race.'"

Bob Wilson was a wonderful guy. He was the best doctor I ever knew and the best friend I ever had. We have lost a man who cared. He's gone too soon.

FIELD NOTES

A small sandpiper seen on 9/29/17, at Force Lake with Tait Anderson and Vanessa. A juvenile bird mixed in with a flock of dowitchers. Clearly smaller than the associated dowitchers and beak only about half the length. warm overall with clearly demarcated rufous cap and bold white supercilium. Buffy breast with minimal streaking and indistinct lower border. white belly.

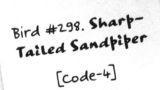

Bird #298. **Sharp-Tailed Sandpiper**

[Code-4]

EPILOGUE

BIRDING UPDATE

Life Totals:

- ABA Area: 673 (including Hawaii)
- Oregon: 405
- Multnomah County: 300

I don't keep a formal world list. It is simply too big a task for someone of my age and health profile. I've probably seen about 1,000 species worldwide. That's a paltry number compared to Iain (for example) who passed 5,000 many years ago and now focuses on owls of the world—he's closing in on 200, an astounding number when you consider that there are only nineteen owl species in all of North America. The list I care about most is Multnomah County. As I was writing this book, I needed just one more bird to reach 300, a total never before achieved by anyone, though all records are made to be broken (I'm thinking of you, Andy Frank). As we were about to go to press, I got number 300, and my dream came true, I got the magical tick.

MEDICAL UPDATE

In recent years I've been spending more and more time at the other end of the stethoscope. ("Life at the Other End of the Stethoscope" ... that has a nice ring to it—a title for my next book?) I'm now more the patient than the doctor. My current medical problem list is as follows:

- Cancer: prostate (2002), bladder (2010), gastric carcinoid (2017). All in remission.
- Cardiovascular: triple coronary artery bypass surgery (2008), carotid endarterectomy (2012), femoral stents (2010, 2016). All stable.
- Neurological: spinal osteoarthritis (2009), idiopathic polyneuropathy (2012), Parkinson's disease (2016). Moderately symptomatic.

But I'm holding my own—still curious, still engaged in the glorious journey, still making the dash in the hope of finding a rare bird. And what am I doing now that I've encountered number 300? I'm looking for 301.

FIELD NOTES

A rather drab warbler discovered on 11/18/17, coming to feeders at the home of Chris Cunningham in NE Portland. The bird was uniformly gray on the nape and upper back, somewhat darker distally but without streaks. Bold white eye-ring best seen in direct sunshine while in a birch tree, less so in shade while at suet feeder. Chest and belly whitish. Yellow on undertail coverts, throat not well seen. Intermittent tail wagging. Seen again on November 20 (tail wagging) and November 21 (best overall).

Bird #299.
Virginia's Warbler

[Mult First Record; Code-5]

ACKNOWLEDGEMENTS

I am grateful to the many people who made significant contributions to the conception and completion of this book. Of special note are Katharine Lawrence, my editor extraordinaire, the other half of spirited debates on all sorts of topics, my right hand; Matthew Fitchen for his expert design of the cover, preparation of the images and design input; and Ellen Fitchen for her loving support and discerning eye.

Many thanks to Joe Kimble, Mary Lawrence, Brett Hyland, and Alan Contreras for their extensive review of the manuscript and thoughtful suggestions; to Shawneen Finnegan for the cover illustration of the Ovenbird, doctored (no pun intended) by Matthew Fitchen; to Nathan Pierce for his incredible drawing of Ivan Mestrovic's statue of the Spearman; and to Dawn Fitchen, Marty Fitchen, and Jane Fitchen for their general support.

In the process of writing this book, I've had the good fortune of reconnecting with people from my past who have helped me verify my recollection of timing and events. These include Zhouman Gardner (Lanakila); Sharon Carroccio (my high school honey); Bruce Grean and George Fleming (Amherst); Ira Shoulson, MD (med school); Jill Goldman (daughter of Bob Goldman, MD); Lou Borucki, MD, Bill Holden, MD, Walt McDonald, MD, Grover Bagby, MD, Scott Goodnight, MD, and Vic Menashe, MD (OHSU); Whit Morriss, MD (my best buddy at USAFSAM) and D. Garon Bailey, lead medical librarian (USAFSAM); Chris Fitchen (T-38 pilot); Mike Riscoe, PhD, and Archie Bauer, PhD (VA Research); Andy Goldstein, Mike Dunton, and Nancy Lime (Epitope); and the guys (Pudknockers).

The birding chapters of this book would not have happened without the help of lots of birders, especially in and around Portland. Notables include Andy Frank, MD (a fellow doctor-birder), Bob Stites, David Mandell, Jim Burns (Wood Sandpiper photograph), Tait Anderson, Art Clausing, and Iain Tomlinson (the best birder I ever met).

To my knowledgeable, friendly, and supportive team at Inkwater Press, especially Virginia Solan, Andrew Durkin, Sean Jones, and Masha Shubin.

FIELD NOTES

Reported to me by Tait Anderson and spotted by me on 9/14/18 on the west side of Sturgeon Lake. A dark juvenile, the bird had an unmistakable jaeger profile and stood calmly in the mud at the fringe of the lake. The bird was very accommodating and allowed me to approach to within fifteen feet. Overall, the bird was dark gray with white highlights. The bill was short with the nail extending halfway back on the upper mandible. Dark around eye. Head and nape pure gray. Crisp white edges on the feathers on the back. Lower abdomen and undertail coverts with striking, transverse black-and-white barring. Legs pale and pinkish in some lighting angles

Bird #300.
Long-Tailed Jaeger
[Mult First Record; Code-5]

FIELD NOTES POSTSCRIPT

Two jaeger species have played a key role in my county birding: a Parasitic Jaeger spotted by me and Iain on Sturgeon Lake on September 25, 2002 (see drawing by Matt Fitchen in Chapter 18). For me, this was Multnomah County Big Year species #201, breaking the record set by Joe Evanich in 1988. And then, some sixteen years later and also on Sturgeon Lake, the Long-Tailed Jaeger shows up for county life list #300. Both sightings made me feel exquisitely happy and deeply reflective, and both remain imprinted in my visual cortex and visceral memory. The big one, #300, was the best—a rare and important bird seen at point-blank range, allowing careful study and certain ID.

BIRD CONSERVATION RESOURCES

American Birding Association
www.aba.org

National Audubon Society
www.audubon.org

American Bird Conservancy
www.abcbirds.org

Portland Audubon Society
www.audubonportland.org

CPSIA information can be obtained
at www.ICGtesting.com
Printed in the USA
LVHW010610170120
643935LV00005B/77